Always Now

Collected Poems
Volume Three

Always Now

Volume One (2003)
From Elsewhere
Winter Sun
The Dumbfounding
Translations

Volume Two (2004)
sunblue
No Time

Volume Three (2005)
Not Yet But Still
Concrete and Wild Carrot
Too Towards Tomorrow: New Poems

Margaret Avison
Always Now ⋘

The Collected Poems
Volume Three

The Porcupine's Quill

Library and Archives Canada Cataloguing in Publication

Avison, Margaret, 1918–
Always now : collected poems / Margaret Avison.

ISBN 0-88984-262-0 (v. 1);   0-88984-255-8 (v. 2);   0-88984-261-2 (v. 3)

I. Title.

PS8501.V5A17 2003   C811'.54   C2003-902232-3
PR9199.3.A92A17 2003

Copyright © Margaret Avison, 2005.
1   2   3   4   •   07   06   05

Published by The Porcupine's Quill, 68 Main St, Erin, Ontario N0B 1T0.
http://www.sentex.net/~pql

Readied for the press by Stan Dragland and Joan Eichner.
Copy edited by Doris Cowan.

All rights reserved. No reproduction without prior written permission of the publisher except brief passages in reviews. Requests for photocopying or other reprographic copying must be directed to Access Copyright.

Represented in Canada by the Literary Press Group.
Trade orders are available from University of Toronto Press.

We acknowledge the support of the Ontario Arts Council and the Canada Council for the Arts for our publishing program. The financial support of the Government of Canada through the Book Publishing Industry Development Program is also gratefully acknowledged. Thanks, also, to the Government of Ontario through the Ontario Media Development Corporation's Ontario Book Initiative.

 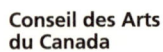 

Volume Three

A Note on the Text   11

Not Yet But Still

Looking Out
   Old Woman at a Winter Window   15
   Beyond Weather *or* From a Train Window   15
   From Now – On?   16
   Contemplative Hour   18
   Lit Sky and Foundered Earth   19
   Thought in a Sick-Room   20
   Not Quite Silently   21
Being Out
   Slow Advance   23
   There Are No Words For   25
   When Their Little Girl Had Just Died   26
   When the Bough Breaks   27
   Knowing the New   28
   Sultry Day   29
   asap; etc.   30
   Making a Living   31
   Air and Blood   32
   Late Perspective   34
   'Tell them everything that I command …'   35
   We Are Not Desecrators   36
   Potentiality   37
Now
   A Peculiarity: Local Loyalties   39
   A Basis   40
   Music Was in the Wind   42
   Communication at Mortal Risk   44
   Poring   45
   Artless Art   46
   Transition   47
   Cross-Cultural *or* Towards Burnout   48

    Cultures Far and Here   50
    The Risk of No Communication   52
    Family Members   54
    A Women's Poem: Now   55
    A Women's Poem: Then and Now   56
    Aftermath of Rebellion   57
    For a Salty and Sainted Friend in Her Nineties   59
    Seer, Seeing   60
    How Open, Who Are Compassed Here?   63

Who

    Concert   65
    The Familiar Friend, But by the Ottawa River   66
    Astonishing Reversal   68
    In Season and out of Season   69
    To Counter Malthus   72
    And If No Ram Appear   73
    What John Saw   74
    Prodded out of Prayer   76
    Embrace Change?   77
    Breath Catching   78
    Proving   79

High Days

    Christmas Doubts Dissolved   81
    Two Perilous Possibilities   82
    That Friday – Good?   84
    Interim   85
    'One Rule of Modesty and Soberness'   86
    It Isn't Really True? (in Four Voices)   90

For the Fun of It

    A Seed of History   93
    Word: Russets   94
    Shelter?   95
    A Kept Secret   96
    Resting on a Dry Log, Park Bench, Boulder   97
    News Item   99
    Instrumentalists Rehearse   100
    Three Bears   101

Job: Word and Action
    Confrontation and Resolution, in *Job*   103

Concrete and Wild Carrot

Pacing the Turn of the Year   119
Present from Ted   122
Towards the Next Change   124
Prairie Poem   125
Dividing Goods   127
Ramsden   129
Balancing Out   130
The Crux   131
Ambivalence   133
Relating   135
Responses   137
Audrey: A Posthumous Portrait   138
Reversing a Crater   139
Third Hand, First Hand   141
Notes from Dr Carson's Exposition of I John 5   142
He Was There/He Was Here   143
Remembering Gordon G. Nanos   144
Other Oceans   146
The Whole Story   155
Cycle of Community   156
Seriously?   158
Dead Ends   159
Prospecting   160
Lament for Byways   161
Rising Dust   163
Two   165
Leading Questions   166
Uncircular   167
The Endangerer   170
To Wilfred Cantwell Smith   171
Four Words: A Gloss on I Cor. 14: 6   173

On a Maundy Thursday Walk   174
In Our 'Little Nests'   176
Contextualizing, *or* Neither Here Nor There   177
Alternative to Riots But All Citizens Must Play   179

Too Towards Tomorrow: New Poems

The Fixed in a Flux   185
Ne Cedere: 'Won't Go Away'   187
Too Towards Tomorrow   189
Resolute Lament   190
Nahuatl/*Tomana* (to Swell)   191
Cosmosis   192
Early Easter Sunday Morning Radio   195
Three Shore Breakfasts   196
Open   197
Ex-Communicants   198
But One Recoiled   198
Because Your Hour Is Dark   199
Ajar   201
Strolling   202
Sad Song   203
The End Not Yet   204
Betrayed into Glory   205
'I Wondered As I Wandered'   206
Loam   208

Acknowledgements   212
Index of Titles   217

A Note on the Text

The three volumes of *Always Now* contain all of Margaret Avison's published books of poetry. The author has removed a very few poems: 'Public Address' (from *Winter Sun*), 'The Two Selves' and 'In Eporphyrial Harness' (from *The Dumbfounding*), 'Highway in April', 'The Evader's Meditation', and 'Until Christmas' (from *sunblue*), 'Living the Shadow', 'Insomnia' and 'Beginning Praise' (from *No Time*), 'Having Stopped Smoking' and 'Point of Entry' (from *Selected Poems*). The opening section of volume one, 'From Elsewhere', is arranged according to date of publication, from 1932 to 1991, the date of *Selected Poems*. 'From Elsewhere' includes the 'Uncollected' and 'New Poems' of that book, except for the two noted above and 'The Butterfly', which is here in its original form. All of the poems in *Always Now* having been considered and reconsidered, and small corrections having been made, the book contains definitively all of the published poems up to 2002 that Margaret Avison wishes to preserve.

Not Yet But Still

Looking Out

Old Woman at a Winter Window

From squared-off quarters
through a frosted pane
I stare into the glittering
quartz of the air, marbled with
tiny streamers from
valiant chimneys down along the valley.

It is as if we pit ourselves
against a congealing It.
We claim these square ceiling and walls
and floor from the immensity
as all that have, for us,
meaning, against the encroaching ice,

the ice that somehow
signals another space, a fearful,
glorious amplitude.

Beyond Weather *or* From a Train Window

Snowflakes in starlight, obliterated into
weft and stippling, buried under
combed sweep and depth, month upon month,
crusting and powdered over,
now – in the gloaming fields – become
round little pools
bright with the lift of the sky they left last autumn.

Mineral beauty. Most such is still
long, for long, hidden.

Looking Out

From Now – On?

The family car has come
for the son who believed
he had left home.
His college luggage heaved
into the back too leaves,
with two of them, still room
in the front seat for him.

Is it his last year?
Where are his companions
to gather and conspire
falsely about reunions?
It's good there's no one there
to witness these old tensions,
old bonds, new fear.

The future closes down
with the slammed trunk.
Dazed by distractions
and like a drunk
awash suddenly with affection
and close to tears, he thinks
of the long-lost home town.

For him, is this disruption?
'An end and no beginning'
now his life's caption?
Ice on bright puddles, birds all singing
to mock the nothingness suction,
the spiritless direction,
his flattened pinions?

In the vague inattention of a too
long life, out walking by
that college: how
many spring term-ends have I
seen the cars load, the shy
parents reclaiming their boy.
And this 'how many' is also,
for me, disruption.

Looking Out

Contemplative Hour

Is there a precious stone somewhere between
pearl-pale and Peace-Rose colour?
not matte, but only subtly
reflecting light?

            It is first light.
The quiet lake four miles away
breathes fragrant peace to this
hill window.
Breathes, not reflects.

Who or what can be
a lake to light, when dark
still muffles the sorrowful thoroughfares?
when worlds of people huddle
heaped up alongside water, everywhere
land once heaved up out of water?

Cities want more window – both to see
and be – though in this last of time,
this early April day
is precious, and not stone.

Lit Sky and Foundered Earth

The nighthawk? no, a gull
far off, only affirms
the quiet of this hour,
as do the children's cries
in the near-dark – still playing,
guilty with freedom, after
this sudden summer on a
school day in October.
Hearing them, you know how
flushed their faces, how
desperate for one last dare:
they listen too for that
voice from a lit window or doorway
to beam them down, and in.

Thought in a Sick-Room

Single leaf shadow
touches leaf
in the still morning window.

The branches of
young leaves (outdoors)
shimmer.

In the eclipse, when I was very young,
someone said – I was a city child –
'Watch it on the pavement
under a big old tree.'

It's true.
Beyond the dot and dash of
less leafy trees
find one in lofted fullness
and the light, in perfect
little sun-round shadows of
itself, falls
on the bald earth – or, in eclipses,
little sun-crescents.

Not Quite Silently

What light of a snow-cloud
here, among us, from where we
stumble along
to as dim far out into the void
as seeing can believe,
can be so overshadowed?

Pale diagrams of snowy
roof levels, and roof angles
rise up out of the smudge
of crouched buildings and
tree-tangle.

The once familiar small things
(normally part of
anybody's day)
blur into the fading of
hill and valley. This somehow
gives all we know a face and
being, though

all, all are muffled, moved
under; moved down into themselves; down
into the unknowable
earth of us all.

Though light is overshadowed, yet the far
comes close, the unknowable
near; the random usual 'here'
is sifted down
feathering eyelid, lashes, blank
eyeball, as if with holy
fear.

Looking Out

Being Out

Slow Advance

One of those tall tall birds
but puce (not
pink as flamingos' pictures are),
high stepping,
> through what seemed the detritus
> of all my city lanes and childhood vacant
> lots – a shadow-casting
> collage of grasses, other (one-legged) people's
> wet socks, odd machine-scraps and
> glass fragments –
> among a few small inky
> patches of rainwater,
draped his slow knee-to-toe
tall tall legs
forward, one by

one. His progress
seemed more significant than memory.

A freshening breeze
teased his shoulder feathers, his
north-sky-coloured shoulders.

More to report would be invention.

Slow, moving, but
with no significant progress,
no furrowing takeoff, ponderous
wing-flapping – was it
the dream-reversal of frenetic motion?

Being Out

For me in my involvement there
perhaps.
But the deliberate purposefulness
of that tall tall
bird was absolute.
Is not a dream.

Being Out

There Are No Words For

when there are no words:
the sweat and clench
of his crescendoing pain
you, helpless, cannot know.

Two together
each quite alone.

Joy too
can single out.
Yes; it aches to be, nonetheless,
always wider in radiance.

Audiences there are
for pain and joy;
some, cold but fascinated,
have comments;
most are involved   look on
helplessly   but
they have no words – even not
for you,
remembering oneness but now frozen out by
that odd proscenium,
privacy, respected.

Having no words is not
safe. It is
then the only good.

Being Out

When Their Little Girl Had Just Died

Does pain prise people apart?
It can.
Who cranks the wedge wider?
No one.
None can give counsel re the split
to two, lopped so, inert,
who shrink from double hurt
(worse, none).

O ocean of known pain
engulf, then, overwhelm
these two into absorption
past all cataclysm
beneath that far pacific line
where pain and joy are one.

Being Out

When the Bough Breaks

Though through the early murk
   the sun, a tangerine ball,
       bulged, briefly,
   the sultry dearth of all
   but grey and remote glower
   is all we're left with.

Soapstone massaged by the faint
   motion of my slowest moving,
I pass a scraggly man
on a park bench, solidly intent
on a black Bible –
     triangled, knees to eyes.
A Chinese grandmother
loiters among twenty-two pigeons on a
glum little square.

City seems loath to stir.
Even the lemon lilies wanly
feel for their little day as if
   it were not now.

Being Out

Knowing the New

The detritus of winter is
hollowed to the rind. But
we find, one day, those old
ridges have vanished, are
washed clean away.

Then for a while
straining anticipation flounders
as every day follows chill day – those
brooding snappish days.

They have passed. Now
even in the city breezes
are gentle with that moist
earth smell.

Suddenly utterance is everywhere.
Little new leaves are
blossomy in frills and lace under the
limpid blue.
And the magnolia has
haloed high around itself a dome
of space,
an eloquent soundlessness
the birds can understand and
re-voice for the wide world.

Sultry Day

It smells like glue.
The bus windows give on
carsheds and
abandoned storefronts.
We do keep breathing
though this vile air.

Pressures are drawing in
however:

Soon there will rise
a sulphur and violet sky.
It will convulse in
fire and water.

Then, with the soiled old world
hosed clean, the blue
windows of light will be
clear, the air
cedar-tip sweet.

asap; etc.

Acronyms, alas,
become words-without-etymology;
components crumble blind;
the agglomerating initials find
themselves picked up by ear without apology
by those too used to symbols without mass.

Are moon and foreheads, and this opening rose
(massively present), nonetheless
the cryptic relics of one word
we know no way to now? have heard
of only in distress
from some original who chose

to spot particulars as part
of utterance, acronymic,
not conceived as final? Sense
and sound of the immense?
fully articulate in a tongue untaught?

Well, that's a place to start.

Making a Living

The industrious young
as if as well carefree
run here at sandpiper gait,
    with the weight of the earth or the
    wavering line of the foam
    from an alien element
    sketching a scalloping path:
they veer and flee and come running
busily, as if carefree.

The old stand hunched,
motionless, like a morning
heron on mist-smoking water standing,
    the way a lightning-crippled oak
    mimicking lightning in its
    old blasted branches
    seems forever bereft of leafing.
Earth under water; sky over all,
waiting; though
there will be, abruptly, a
brief tussle: life, from death.
Another fast is broken.

Being Out

Air and Blood

The beautiful Tuesday morning
light is refined by the
haze of
metropolis, breathing.

Away out there in the pitiless
clarity of field and riverflats,
one by one, in an odd
kind of despair,
countrymen, the young, torn but
compelled, throw off
pitchfork and pieties,
shoulder belongings, hit the road.

The bus slews to a gravelly stop
just up the grade. He runs,
bundle joggling. Aboard
is the metropolis's
breathing, but not here
refined.

From private acres, near and far away,
somehow a diaphragm seems to be in an
agglomerative rhythmic
tilting, dislodging, sloughing off.

Now!

Feverish, at first
exhilarating, seems
the energy,
the beauty even –
as, on this beautiful Tuesday, morning
light is refined by
the haze of megalopolis.

Being Out

Late Perspective

Ribbed sand under clear shallows,
    stray, shadow-probing pebbles,
        receive the quiet light.

Changed
      since under the soundless
    weight borne deep under ocean,
    the boil and hiss, and there
    sealed off, hardened, still
    unresisting, massively shouldered out
    and moved by those
    terrible forces that grind
    down, grind down,
this shore-pan suffers now the mild
face of the morning.

Long we stand listening here.

Then the children are brought and, quickly
prancing up shells of water, they
muddle the parallel patterns of the sand
along the stippled shallows,
reckless – why should they not be? – of the ancient
touches that grit on their
spade handles, their
tender ankle skin,

and eons' flow slows to the
intermittent droplets of
their morning's timeless time.

**'Tell them everything that I command you;
do not omit a word' (Jer. 26: 2b)**

Night? barely past noon?
An eerie quiet, then
the crack and rustle of fear.

But in that hour
just before the storm/doom
crashed down,

with force and immediacy, heard
by every child, woman and man,
came the word, spoken
through Jeremiah who
moved past darkness.

Yes, they had heard
his long-range forecasts.
But now, they knew, believing now
had them closed in with seeing.

Being Out

We Are Not Desecrators

After a noisy night of rain
sun comes flooding. Droplets shine
on every blade of grass and curl of budding
leaf. Under the young
maples, under the cloud and sunpour,
tree-meal spreads its saffron glow.

Silenced almost is the city's endless
snoring, our kettledrum activity
(one playing field away).

My kind out there sullies
it all, as I do being here.

Yet we, providing an unlikely
context for miracle, maybe, alone,
are inwardly kindled.
(The songsparrows, for instance, are
wholly given to improvising their
immemorial singing – further
compelling us despoilers
to pure awareness!)

Also, the night was no surprise.
This morning, with its opening skies,
is.

Through the preempted hours
and all our outs and ins, there stir
long-lost rememberings
of sudden summer. New
antiphonal vistas open.

Being Out

Potentiality

Humble is the intensity of
a seed.

It lies there
too small to cast a shadow,

as the invisible is too large, compassing
light and shadow both;

yet there is
a bond that makes them one.

Now

A Peculiarity: Local Loyalties

If only I were a farmer
I would put this better. But

suppose a salesman drives in and
strolls around to find
where you are working, and sees
your ripening apples, the aging
trees (but sturdy)
(the young orchard is all
spindle and tracery still),
and says:

'This product we prepare
from our own research
will swell your fruit by four
times, and redden its cheek
to make it more enticing
to the public.'

                You stand listening.

Your dad once said,
'Son, never trade
flavour for show.
Offer something choice.
Fewer may want it, but in the course
of giving them quality you're giving
yourself incentive, and satisfaction –
just about enough, at the day's end.'

So you clear your throat, and send
him away with a shrug, and an apple in his hand.

                            Now

A Basis

*Preface. This is about
many of us. You deride
the stereotype of my peculiar
subculture? That would be good-
bye to something you might want understood.*

The missionary 'call'
is part expulsiveness.
In all, in Antioch,
stresses through Paul, the saint
(despite that gentle 'encourager' on his team)
may have begun to fray a seam or two.
They, moved to send them out,
welcomed the Spirit's 'Go',
thankfully left on their own then, to 'work out
their own salvation', having forced themselves to
'go' themselves in order to stay.

Am I accusing Paul
of a short fuse? of chafing
on a short leash? Was he
a venturesome unsettler? Where he went,
restlessly, on and on,
his stays established outposts of the
heavenly imperium which must
in turn disrupt all empires. Saints galore
experienced then the senders'
stresses, unsettlings, frayed seams;
but also they experienced
the saint's propulsive
fire in the bones, although operative
in followers now, the leader
first demonstrated and then
taught and, yes, enforced

>   Now

following as his
own freedom, and as theirs – and ours.

So an expulsive Paul
was after all the heartbeat of heaven's purposes?
But was the hard-driven church
in Antioch at fault?
Was the word ('Send forth!')
mistranslated in some of their hearts
as 'Let's get rid of'; a prayer even: 'Relieve
us of the gad-
fly in our sweetest ointment? Leave,'
perhaps they thought, 'that we may live
sheltered but no more driven by our faith.'

Faraway saints become dear to
the here unthreatened.

Most threads are twisted.
They tend to knot. I.e. the best
must be, on earth,
only the worst in course of
being transfigured.

Disruptive change could not
be hindered.
Nor can it. Surrendered to
impulse some venturers may go
alien ways – were these galling at home?
    Expelled? Sent? Summoned?

The outcome is the same,
there and even here.

                              Now

Music Was in the Wind

It was Orpheus all along!
He carried Eurydice down, down
into the earth
in his arms, going himself with her
since this was the only way
out of her mortal maze now.
All he had then he risked
except a love strong and steady enough
never to share her
relief in this fine-sifted silence, nor
her torn
loyalties to this private place
and to the devastated but remembered
home where she was known.

First it had to be down.
He was no
stoic, no ascetic, moved to
goodness without experience
of all our billion moments. Did he
hear what the shepherds overheard?
sweet singing in the choir?

He carried her he loved
the whole way down.

The strange travail home
up into light
emptied his arms. He
took her by the hand, and she was walking.
And on the way they would be
sometimes sensitive to a loss as she
lived it out in a familiar

Now

and yet an altered world,
remembering a morning, in a song,
going about the city in the streets,
yet even then
knowing him once again beyond our wall:
'Arise, and come....'

Communication at Mortal Risk

The prow of that icebreaker
was a person.

The channel is still open.
It must be kept so.

Another person is already
in place. Others
are primed.

> *Surely this deadly rescue*
> *must not go on.*

This channel is our
local concern;
there are others even
more, or as, vital;

these concern us
deeply too. But here we must
keep at it while
someone still can.

Poring

These words* become
opaque when wrestled down.
They're plain but ponderous
with pastness.

Yet there begins to
emerge – see! – far,
farther: a distinct design,
like miniature landscapes in the sun
out through the arch in a Gozzoli
painting.

Out of the numbing
pastness opens an – escape!
an invitation? One expects
to breathe that light
somehow, and perhaps see
even the grassblades, and the
shadows of the grassblades.

---

*E.g., in Leviticus

Artless Art

When we were children, who
did not contrive
a secret language? – nobody 'else' to know
the key, for ever.

By now
both of us have, I guess,
written it out
plain, in the common tongue. We
know, though, that the secure
never will decipher it.

But to one another we,
here and there, are known,
all marvelling at the
how-it-is-said
so that the what
still scarcely matters.

Transition

When they ransacked
the ancient memory
some became learned
and the learning became dust;
some would have bartered
their loot. But
found out in the market
it had all
become fools' gold.

The hollowed ancient places
echoed with silences.

The tension rises
through the snowlight of the
dark hours. Cut off.
And listening past
possibilities.

Odd, that such yearning wonder
should, for fear
turn to ice.

                                        Now

Cross-Cultural *or* Towards Burnout

Your rage is bearable as your
swallowed insults and the limp
collusion with us were not
to you, were to us echoes only of
our inauthentic guilt.

Yet your rage hurts.
A post-colonial white woman, I am
therefore a thing-hog,
easy taker-for-granted, helpless
to unmake the bed
others made for me, even before
grandpa (and even he was
simply another fellow working long hours,
kindly, respectful, whether paid or not).
And I lie, tossing, in that
incontestably comfortable bed.

What has been crafted in behind
green hedges of 'our heritage'
took centuries, took lives.
It formalized, in time, our
savage sorrow into this
chamber music. We need
a life half-lived-out, maybe more
to be constrained to music in
quiet fullness of sorrow.

We are outraged at your
raw grief, at
the bony barricades of
borne indignity:
your five-year-old coming in,
defeated, facing still
another day of what   Now

our five-year-old will say and do.

Through Jeremiah I had
faced up to God's fierce anger.

Therefore your rage is the
long held under
knowledge of the holy child's
knowledge of
the spittle, the
flogged back, the suave
manipulator's deathly mockery,
present, every wracked
generation, as if helplessly.

Your work is dark and bitter.

Ours, rounded up at last from the
once fortress city, picking our way
out through its rubble, bound
for forced labour in remote Asian
cities, or
slavery in
others' mansions and palaces.

Our God endures.

The sentinel trees
on a far hilly ridge
remind us of perennial
destruction, restoration, on
wave lengths much too vast to ease
you and the child today
or us into tomorrow.

                                                Now

Cultures Far and Here

or rich and poor?

One voice, one looming face, first,
one floor and roof,
windows on daylight, and (when the
wonder must be tracked)
out in the windy grass
or along cliffs,
or through the steamy lowlands
I've never seen, with leaves
as large as elephant ears,
or in a secret cove
safe from the thundering surf –

these and the strangeness
of meeting a potential friend
with different memories
to travel with,
and others, more, confronting sometimes:

all these early imprintings give us
person by person
our natures, each unique as fingerprints.

That's frightening. We cluster
telling each other
stories that build the vault of a
shelter from the wholly
unknown, comforted by what
is recognizable in our overlapping
awareness.

Now

But sky and weather
have a way of disregarding our
walls, sweeping us on to
not being an 'us'.

Out there it's larger
every time we're stripped
of almost everything familiar.

If it were violent exposure
it would be less
insidious. Because it's featureless
the wide starless daylight is
vacuous.

East-west, equator-outwards, people
scramble like flotsam, and the tides
wash out all little dunes and bays and
private promontories.

Now

The Risk of No Communication

X: 'To "interface" I'll go
out under rainstripped trees
among the ones who
hurl up their sticks and choose
the shiniest chestnuts, squinting at the sky.

Or in the amber city go
among the fruitstalls and the cheese
markets, mashing down the
greens and sawdust on the walkways,
alert for the particular face
never before, nor since, seen, open,
even responsively human
for an instant, as we carry our
different faces on into
each his own life.'

A: 'No. No. To interface
　is to bring the parties' two
　predicates to contrive a
　single new
　composite terminology.
　The mix may spur
　ideas, shift perspectives, even
　highlight some overlooked potentiality.'

X: 'A factoring down?
Cutting mutual losses? never
facing one another?
(Face. Faces. Etymology:
"face" – 'a making', *cf* "sur-faces").'

Now

X's Younger Friend: Such Latin roots
have become marginal. What roots
nurture the desiccation of language now?
with wires as good as stems?
Structure will be secure in their
designing hands.

Now

Family Members

The tethered dory thuds
in its lonely sarabande
after the speedboat's passing.
Thuds on the dock, as gradually
criss-crossing wavelets
scallop the weathered piles.
Thud. Then bump. Then nudge.

Wood shaped to shel-
ter even the clumsiest oarsman,
shaped to cumber
the sundanced waters or
the still angora mists of dawn.
Wood of the dock, wet fibring
wood piles solid on rock
fixed in cement – knee-deep
in a dry autumn, hip-deep and standing steady
when March foments the slush to gnaw
and no one sees or listens.

Wood, tied to wood,
but not by wood and
only in waiting intervals;
each mostly on its own.

Now

A Women's Poem: Now

Women are breadwinners perforce
when their pay is their sole resource.
Or when couples aspire to arrive
at a house – not a cell in a hive.

Santa Lucia was practical
too. Only after betrothal
to a rich man did she share her
dowry, all of it, with the poor.

Someone (her husband?) suspected
her Christ-act, and to correct it
let the Roman prosecutor
pursue the matter, and martyr her.

A Women's Poem: Then and Now

Some people couldn't care less
how they dress.
A few resolve to wear
only what was someone else's before.

Most people like to shop.
They never stop,
and smile if something fits – and is reduced.
They buy the mass-produced.

One or two let salons present
them well, for each event,
uncaring about cost, keeping in mind
that theirs is one-of-a-kind.

In this new age the fashion
is wearing a used person.
An emperor's clothes, in artless ostentation?
Why 'reincarnation?'

Why contemplate it, over
a name, unique, forever?
Before opting for evil – and shame and flight –
Adam and Eve went naked in the full light!

Now

Aftermath of Rebellion

When runners came with news
after the Battle in the Forest
the King's hopes stirred – here was
no rout, no loyal remnant
straggling home to defend
an indefensible throne.

Yes, the first praised the Lord his God
(the King's), obviously glad in
the monarch and his kingdom
made secure. Yet
(and hope flickered):
'What of Absalom?'

The second, the official slower
runner, with a word
stifled the air and
hope went out.

'Would God that *I* had died for *him*.'

The father's lament
has lingered on the ancient air of grief
at least till now.

A vain, muscular, risk-defying,
fine-looking heir to
prospects that one day would
amaze the Queen of Sheba,
a rebel, a contemptuous
underminer, had flung off

Now

– forever now –
in his young man's euphoria,
his father's hand.

For such a delinquent
even, a sovereign, sick at heart,
learned what it is when
a father loves.

For a Salty and Sainted Friend in Her Nineties

She had survived Intensive Care
but still valiantly hoped
to escape hospital or what-
ever new way-station,
e.g. a nursing-home.

'It saved your life,' said the doctor.
'Saved – from what?' She
wryly rebukes his jauntiness
at having intervened. Her eyes are
snapping with conviction and –
amusement.
Almost disdainful of death, she
presses him, 'From what?'

'No,' her granddaughter
gently puts in,
'not from, saved for
another not-too-difficult
year or so perhaps? or for
mornings like this, quiet, with the
lilac and white lilac
dimness of it? for
some unpredictable …?'

Well, maybe (grudgingly
conceded). But, 'Saved –
for what?' And let
the patient answer.

Now

Seer, Seeing

I am no cow of Bashan, Amos.
No. I'm not poor, for all I've tried to end up
understanding that, by being it.
It didn't work. I work.
My meals are
ordinary, and by no means
easily shared in
fact – though gestures can
make maybe some
trifling difference somewhere.

    The scale is huge now, but
    the story still the same,
    all this more-than-millennium later.

    It's hemispherics we talk now
    or off and on emergency relief
    (we're bothered, even generous.)
    Our 'world' still has
    palaces, malls, temples, do-goodery
    and make-goodery – institutionalized.

Institutions have all the words, but
there's not an institution speaks for
you, or for me hearkening for you,
any more than for

    her, left alive, with listening eyes
    sitting amid a strew of
    bodies where a passing gust
    ruffles, idly.

    These were that 'other half'
    that is no longer half a world away.

                                        Now

We worked for, dreamed for, this;
    or worked to live, and ended building this
structure, made from traditional
materials of the first excellence.
What is your quarrel, Amos?

       Tear down
       Tear down.

They will? We?
Institutions rainbowed like soapsuds
in bonny air are bursting, superseded
by predators
out to hunt down the all too much that
is no more.

You fulminated, released to
sweep all before the
tides of holy anger.

Then, Amos, you end up with
bucolic bliss!

       As though perennial contentment
       were bedded down on everyone
       else's fetid
       declension into formlessness!

       Din into my ears
       your dirge, Amos. Set my last
gaze on
a whole people convulsed, roam where they
may,
horizon to horizon to horizon.

                                   Now

I cannot yet
see, my vision blurred by vapour trails,
riot-torn cities' smoke,
hot breathings from cored mountains,
oh, by the too-late industries
        puncturing pre-sunset smog
        seeking too late to trans-
        mogrify tropical and
        other swarming nowheres to
        spitefully replicate club men and
        women and their
        clubs and memories.
And yet I see you
        banking on seed and
embers and all through
        the world of bombast and
        frozen-eyed bewilderment,
        and torn inside too
        by your own torrent of words,
        all through, you resolutely breathed in
        sun and rain's sweetness
        with simple joy,

        and not just in that
        curious coda, that halcyon aftermath,

but all through, all the way through
with a true hunger banking on
one sturdy today
until tomorrow is today, until
the one with no tomorrow.

Now

How Open, Who Are Compassed Here?

Guessing what the world
will be when we
develop multi-faceted
eyes, like flies',
unsteadies its slow girth
sweeping from west
to east, trailing its
skies.

                                        Now

Who

Concert

Learning, I more and more
long for that simplicity,
clarity, that willingness
to speak (from anonymity ...)
all those impenetrables, when words
are more like bluebell petals under
an absorbed heaven.

You fret because the underbrush
is dense, the way uncleared it seems
where you now find yourself?

Words have been given. Once.
Words that are storm and sun and rain.
Listening earth, where they have fallen,
finds seed casings begin
to split,
roots throb. As though
some unimaginable response is
implicit in that speaking.

Fulfilment is in promise
and still more resonant longing.

The Familiar Friend, But by the Ottawa River

The person addressed is Judas Iscariot. The words centuries later reflect a possible train of thought in the human mind of his human-divine friend whom he would betray. And die of it.

River, enriched in the last light:
this is the cool of the day.
Calm and close, all together,
no one needs words, the
stillness brimming, like those
muscular waters in the lingering light.

And did I plan
before you chose to come?
or after, for that matter, when we were
at peace, breathing companionability
together?
But there were fleeting
expressions, wordless mealtimes
and I could know that that
uninterrupted unemphatic
walking the roads, the hills, would generate
exasperated wonder-
ing about something ... else,
before the marking of time
(and it was sure), somebody ...
else who would
not be all-encompassing.

I knew I am the one
you one day, towards
evening, would
leave. You had prepared for
what had to happen.

                                                             Who

When it did it burned
deeper than your mind.
Nothing will medicine the sore
but an abiding with the wordless glory –
mirroring waters flowing.

If only memory were not
one function of mind.

Astonishing Reversal

In holiness alone
is freedom.

My skeins come twisted to
my hands – I see
another's frayed; tangled
too much to not be broken.

The holy one, who seemed to
put us all in constraint
by being –
why! all along –
will not be banished from
room or field or cockpit or
anywhere we are, is

patiently, alone,
fingering the snarls and
stringing out the one-by-one
way of liberation.

In Season and out of Season

Today the blueness burns
inbetween new greens and space's
soundless blackness.
Yet we even now
discern more, cry:
No, lovely as May is
we would hear more.

>   Moses, you are the voice
>   the Voice spoke with.
>   Centuries have not, will not,
>   still that, therefore. The marvel
>   of the pitched cradle of reeds, the appeal
>   to a ruler-murderer's daughter's
>   mothering heart, the barter
>   of true for foster care that became both;
>   your growing,
>   that unexceptional miracle
>   of years: it all made way for
>   what? One small pure drop –
>   anticipation? hope? – hung on life's
>   strange leaf-edge; trembling in the light
>   for years, for all your years indeed,
>   for 'By faith Moses …'.* It is said.

Exult in warmth and depth
of branches here? Yes, and yet Antarctica
in this same season,
snarls, pounces, gnaws – even while
today the earth
rejoices in deliverance in this zone.

---

* Heb. 11: 24.

Who

> Moses, your early privilege turned
> when you saw abuse into
> an alienating cause? What burned
> was not the authorities' heartless
> indignation, not
> the mute slaves', not
> even your own
> violent indignation, in the end.
> Bare-soled on desert sand
> you bowed,
> and bartered with your seclusion for
> your people's whole concern,
> the Other's deep concern,
> finally given to both.

For many days
here, a sagging cloud and stiff
dark mat of branch and twig,
clacking, entombed us all. Now that winter's over
the trees and shrubs are thimbleberried with
chestnut flowers, with deep-breathed lilacs.

> Moses, how does your solitary death –
> and you went up the lonely crags
> as bidden –
> follow? Did the Voice
> seek silence then? from faith
> were you led … further?
> It may be heaven is the
> light that … conceals?

Your longing then was
not so much to
realize the Land for you were
sure about the Land
long since by faith,
but to be brought
where the celestial Other would
be known in fullness
however dark?

He saw the Lord. He, Moses, was seen
transfigured too, in mountain light, when
much was made plain by once
caring enough to pray to be
blotted out.
(For he had stood among his
fractious, protesting people; he
recognized too his own
moment of failure to
stand with the Voice, heeding instead
an unholy flare of
exasperated nature. Once. Enough.)

Not in season, in the revolving solar system, in which we turn
changeably, always.
Not without the appalling
lightless depth. Not but as a way station
perhaps   is the
unimaginable light where
all maybe is plain.

Who

To Counter Malthus

None of us in this so
burdened earth has known
how to live, let alone
who is too many.

Presence, each day
afresh, you give a
purifying signal to
sting us alive.

Vast territories and seashores
still bear these thronging
strangers. May none die
without somebody caring.

To know even one other is
costly. And being known.
Alive, among so many
more now? a concern …

Hunger makes men desperate, threatens
to congeal the quandary. Yet
Presence abides untouched
in the churn of Quantity.

And If No Ram Appear (Gen. 22: 13)

I saw a father fudge on his first love
when a loved child,
> born in a family of faith
> in a world no longer in sympathy,
> born of an ancient lineage –
> only a stigma, here –
mattered more, in a moment of decision.

John 3: 16
sang out, suddenly:
the only-begotten yielded up, the father
steadied by a harshly
beautiful, and implicit, priority,
with his whole heart
willing:

> goodness made real on earth,
> put within possibility, so that,
> by choice, an answering love
> could make complete the circuit. Shame became
> resplendence
for the priority stands.

Break open every sin of ours
this way! from a broken heart
forgiveness opens out,
more, finding
we matter. And how much.

Who

What John Saw (Revelation 4)

The black holes out there, of pure (physical) force
in the heavens,
those in-and-out plosions, focused,
remote, in a rhythm of
incomprehensible infrequency
but nonetheless in time,
speak the extremes absolute of a rhythm
we mortals know.
They are like us contained in
creation's 'Let it be so.'

Who can comprehend, with a heart hungry
for meaning?
who does not feel the uprooting
tremor of one event –
one person's, or, in the stupefying
astronomers' book of hours, one
pulse of the megalorhythm?

Yes   yes   I know
this bronzing beech tree, the
blackening myrtle at its foot
(event in all my seasons,
seasoned for this long before I was
born) exists in a mere
twitch, is rushing towards the node
millennia away, and that just one
of many, just one episode.
Time curls on itself.

Least moments given, though,
can open onto
John's comprehender: here,

Who

there, then, always
now, because unchanging, who
made light and ponderous rhythms, time, and all
pulsing particulars.
John saw him rainbowed in glory –
compact of all our music, hearing the farthest
compositions, and the most intricately
present. Magnet. Intensifier. Agonizingly
rediscovering, in shards, the shapes
design is satisfied to see.
One.   White.   Whole.

Secret within
all that John saw
is the bronzing beech tree
of this October twilight
though I do not yet see,
even in mind, being
not yet out of time.

Who

Prodded out of Prayer

Stilled yet by
the gauzed withdrawingness of
midmorning sky:

lo, a sharply lit
acutely poignant
and wonderfully humorous
vision.

It was an ant
towing a grass-blade
in a bee-line, but on
rougher terrain,
to the anthill.

Who

Embrace Change?

Embrace? But he will
never draw near for long, would never
choose to pause here.

All right, all right,
I'm panicking.
                He's at my door.

Am I a
recommended B and B?

And though the door
opens only as far
as the chain, through the toe-edge
in the last light, I see
too much of elsewhere to be safe.

Shivering, I say no.
And he says nothing as he turns away.

Breath Catching

The one day will require
all times to be full.
There are no corners.
A beloved stranger
has gone
whose reappearing
spells apprehension, panic,
all we have to hang on to.

Proving

'… do not omit a word' (Jer. 26: 2b)

Truth speaks
all things into being.
No word more, but
not one left unspoken.
Truth carves, incises,
to the bone,
and between bone and marrow.
No wonder
we want none of him.
The wonder is
truth loves;
died of it, once.

Truth lives.
Acting on what is spoken,
not a syllable extra,
nothing omitted,
brings into being
just what is prophesied.
That is the test –
not of what has been spoken
but for the hearer,
his act.

Who

High Days

Christmas Doubts Dissolved

The mayfly's day is significant for
God and that mayfly,
and mine yours his hers
to God, and each such 'me'.

God's little bodily birth is
absolutely unique,
distinct from what he chose
as our particularity.
It's in one flick of time's eternal eye
known, but not evidentiable
(there's what his mother told the
historian years later, but even he
traces a patrilinear descent –
having declared the virgin's miracle).

Were it all otherwise
would the point be, for the mayfly,
and for me, so
poignantly permanently new?

Two Perilous Possibilities

He was a discard, 'bearing the disgrace'.

Graciously (me too in the raggle-taggle)
summoned to join him there, we're set to 'praise
continually'. That is our 'sacrifice'
bringing to equipoise his shame.

This on a drizzly December
midday staggers belief. Cement trucks lumber
past, on a muddy street.
Crowds jumble by, their faces
preoccupied, or strained, or smiling oddly, some
numbly conditioned to hurt. The number
of us, just in itself, disheartens from
crediting supernova-to-small-town-Alberta
focus on one
or the required crescendo
of that much 'praising'
one by one.

But he is there still 'bearing the disgrace'.

Is this perhaps the day before – his table-
settings in place – he will summon
us the street people, us the straggle
of refugees and buskers and all
odds and sods – since thus
honoured guests are provided
his way? The preferred guests
whom we had honoured
had to be superseded (for,
they said, their own sakes).

High Days

Or is it still December
before again a new
genesis for one of us
because the focus still is on
one in 'disgrace'
risking the end truly to
make it new?

High Days

That Friday – Good?

At least the twentieth century is ending.

Wretched insignificant
hurt-all-over all-through
is all there is.
Alone in the universe

and even then (feebly) the 'Why?'

>   Someone, if present,
>   would make it go back to before
>   or at least make it better?

That's not true.

Abandoned.

>   What if the someone
>   were to be, every sinking moment,
>   were to have been,
>   present, all along?

You mean – that's true?

Interim

Easter trumpets, lilies, clamouring
in a blare of sun
rejoice the few, leave many wondering
what, here, heralds the One

who is one with, distinct from, Him
whose word and its outworking
they tried to seal in stone.
Does love still call Him? to long-suffering?

within our death-time? In the morning
pallor of waters, He has come
to vanish – out of human reach, yet waiting
quietly to be known.

Our troubled faces clear to see Him, being
radiantly here, somehow between
familiar days and what's beyond imagining.
We cannot take it in.

Our severed lives are blundering
about in what's been done,
appalled, exultant, sensing
freedom, we seem alone,

but doggedly set out, against a sting
of rain, moved by His plan,
through night and shale-blue dawn, remembering
at least to follow on.

High Days

'One Rule of Modesty and Soberness'

(Calvin, on angels, *Institutes* I, xiv, 4)

How to talk about, being mortal,
angels, an angel become
angels?

We want to distract ourselves
    with the sky-thirsting
        saplings of April
or with the so long motionless
pale eggs now wounded with the wobbly
life within them.

Near. In the aftermath, too.
A stupefying brilliance
felled the young guards
yet the mild voice was factual, gentle, with
the laden mourners at a deserted tomb
in the first light of a new era.

Our mortal memory structures
in us what matters – to
bury it, or
re-celebrate so as to
falsify it: we are
made less than the angels, said the ancient
poet, who knew.

    In their remembering it is now:
    wingrush and choiring and joy
    on the shepherds' hill for their
    Shepherd, newborn, nearby, for their
    finding and love.

High Days

But now also the darkness
at the third hour has not been able to
obliterate what (except, O woe, to
mortals) is
unthinkable....
Having to know that
darkness is a kind of non-
being for these, an arrest, a stared-at
blank. The resonant
eyes within them must have been
charred, then....

That was, to us humans,
thinkable?

Yes. We do it.
We taunt the promise of hope,
wanting the innocent to
turn and twist like us,
goading him to that end
as though every twist and cruel jibe
he had not already
deliberately absorbed, becoming a
death to be
died to
indeed.

So can a mortal
capable of such violation of such
light, approach the heart of what
that darkness is, to
those pure spirits who are in God's
presence always? who are always
coming and going for

High Days

purposes that our heartbreaking
'NO' blacked out, those three long days?

Peter made known that 'even
angels long to look
into these things'.*
But would the poise of holy nature
be disruptible as is our nature's?

   More likely the
   angel, angels,
   contained, brimmed with, their total pain in
   undemanding quietness.

Not these messengers brought on
the geological convulsion;
nor was the lightning shock
their instantaneous signal.
But unbelief's swift 'NO'
wracked earth; mortals resort to
blocking out that way.

   The angel was, the two
   were, merely
   realizing some of the dead man's
   last words, lucidly
   explaining: he will keep his word.
   Expect him.

Only the breath of dawn-
drenched air moves.

---

* 1 Pet. 1: 12.

High Days

Silence even is music, with
the pressure of *glorias* on
misereres on a threshold of
terrible exaltation.

They found its only release: absorption in
his words, their embassy,
and the new future borning.

High Days

It Isn't Really True? (in Four Voices)

'Attention!
This is not your pilot speaking.

Your pilot is out of control.
Your plane is
crashbound. Attention!
Hear me. Quiet, please,
those of you who hear me
and would rather not be hearing me.
Most will not hear or know until
not even risk remains,
only finality. *You* I am here to direct.
Move quietly to the rear.
Thank you, two, three of you.
Please do as I say, as
you see them doing, you fearful ones.
You will all transship.
I will be in control of the
air suction forces on
ejection, and reboarding.
Yes, in mid-air. You can
trust me: see that round hatchway
low, to your left? It did not
appear till now; the
steward is unaware of it.'

Roar of blinding blood in the ears,
tumult, an interval like freefall
and white noise. And

    'Look! It's the arrival corridor
    of an airport.

High Days

The luggage carousel – I'm
meeting someone there.
I know, we left it all....'

    'The flight is in!
    It didn't crash!'

'But we *did* go
out that hatch....
We were looked after, somehow.
Somehow ... don't you feel
looked after, still?'

    'Yes but
    "crashbound", the same voice said.'

'Maybe he meant
some other kind of ending?'

        'Attention!
        All passengers from Flight x99
        arriving from Dorval,
        please reclaim your carry-on
        luggage. Report to Airport Lost and Found
        before leaving the terminal. *Attention!*'

    'Did that other voice
    do it bilingually?'

'No. At least, two or three
of us seemed to
understand.'

                        High Days

For the Fun of It

A Seed of History

One brilliantly cold Alberta day
the teacher wrote on the blackboard
'1928' – for the first time. Everything was changing
so that the blue-and-pink map of Canada
still on the wall was a welcome
constant, in the excitement of this
January newness.

We wrote it on our papers
in round big shapes,
Jan., 1928.

The snow outside
glittered like mica-shavings
in the Alberta sunshine.

Word: Russets

Whoever longs for spring to come,
be stayed by winter's hamper-hued
but choicest – russet apples.

Though it still feel iron hard
its seeds are black, its juices sweet.

Aroma? in the seeds?
There is a fragrance of the one-day flower;
later, a tang of fruit; sharper in peel.
But – seeds?

Where else is the aroma hid?
and how much more of good
sensed, anticipated,
or understood.

For the Fun of It

Shelter?

There's a door in
to the tree,
to the hillside,
to yesterday's home
(they've changed the knocker),
in to the
boathouse-loft snow must have
borne lopsided now
in one corner.

Outdoors, in
under the raftering dusk,
the smoke-red sun
finds an incisive scraggle of
brush on its last
low hill,
signalling time to go
in.

A Kept Secret

One day there flew
from greengold shadows here to those
indigo shadows
deeper among the trees,
in a trice, fanning light,
your wide sky-combing pinions
encompassing, in a breath,
both dark and dazzling.

Each was comprehended and
simply, in equipoise,
contained.

The dark was not
Thomas Hardy's, not
the West's gaunt watershed:
bedaubed everyman, ducking
from any horizon.

Darkness is changed
once it is comprehended; it becomes
knowledge, beyond our reach.

And the flash
stirred by your flight – and gone –
still startles. What does anyone
know of light?

Something to weigh, until
the branches become black
against the amber evening.

Resting on a Dry Log, Park Bench, Boulder

I love to see birds walk.
Oh yes of course, their singing,
their soaring, their
flocking in autumn branches, their
unerring drift down onto a
wire, a tassel of pine:
all these delight.

But that a bird
comes simply among us,
steps as we must (though some,
sandpipers, robins, etc.,
like children bob or run)
touches us.
        They come for seeds
           or crumbs perhaps, a comfortable
touching down we can well understand
although for us to
'consider the birds of the air' in this regard
can be uncomfortable.
        But play is part
        of any living creature's
        energy.

I like to think birds walk
for fun. They trust
another element awhile
as a child wades in snowdrifts.
I have seen delicate patterns
of bird tracks in
deep snow, where only particles of manna
could be there for them, for the drifts
were deep, too deep for grasses, and

                                        For the Fun of It

there were no shrubs,
and people's footsteps there were none.

Nor were there the faint fanning
traces of wings, on takeoff.
Did they jump first, then fly?

> Give me no explanations. If a biologist
> finds talk of walking birds a
> blurring of distinctions, an outsider's
> invasion of a territory
> with its own necessary laws, and language,
> I respect him or her for that,
> especially if this old joke
> makes us both smile:

> A pigeon was late meeting
> a friend at City Hall –
> 'It was such a fine day,' he said,
> 'I thought I'd walk.'

For the Fun of It

News Item

Today, May 9th,
the chestnut trees
pagoda'd in full
seven-fold leaf
out of a blue sky.

Instrumentalists Rehearse

Fishes off on cruises
dream, staring up to sky.

Maple keys let themselves be
sodden and mashed down
into the earth. Their biddable eyes
still towards the trusted
nurturer's, without
any idea what
'fruitful' may turn out to mean
(one papery inch from lofted leafiness!)
– or 'multiply'.

Planets and constellations
dance to like music
not needing to know that
their lost millennia will
shine in a fledgling owl's
eyes in the dark forest deep
deep in the heart of
their fathomless night.

Three Bears

Three polar bears
on a pink ice floe
dance round slow-
ly revolving under
the teal-blue Arc-
tic red-rimmed circle of sky.

Music icicles
picket them round
soundlessly
the dancers three.

They swivel high-
er and higher still
till nobody else was left at all.

Job: Word and Action

Confrontation and Resolution, in *Job*

Proem

Devastation is the seed-bed
for a new era.
Fifteen months of flood waters
recede at last.
Lazarus dies with the saver of lives
summoned, not responding
in time.
John the Baptist grimaces from
Salome's salver.
Jerusalem's stones and golden
ritual vessels
become flesh and blood, and
know it, in
rubble and in
time.

A Book Review

Idle to do this.
Nothing will do
but to read the book.
For one thing, it is
immeasurably better,
and clearer, and probably more accessible.

Why write about it then?
Because I want to,
to cope with it
in human company.

Job: **Word and Action**

Words written down
centuries and many centuries
ago in a
faraway land, were properly
special and enigmatic
in some ways
to be studied and pondered. I
thought. And found
the reading put me in
the midst, not as the self I knew
and certainly not by being manipulated into another's
identity, but –
on purpose.
I found myself belonging
without surprise, in a new setting.

Anyone who reads this book
risks losing forever any belonging that
he thought defined himself.

Stop here and read the book, if you
want that, not just
a book review.

The Subject

Job was a good man.
His biographer gives a
picture of parental and
political reliability.

When Job refers to his own life
and doings, he elaborates;
the account squares with his three friends'
opinions too.
He was a good man.

(It's not a usual situation
for someone to
define in action what he knows is
perfect polity.)

The Context

If Job did what he said –
and I believe him when he
said it, only because
by then his back was
up against the wall –
if in the dismissive eye
of all the disbelievers, also
facing himself, even then,
he said it,
anyone would believe:

> he had not once
> failed a hungry man or a
> defenceless child or an
> abandoned woman or
> the stranger at his door.

If he did give what it took
always (and yet
he also said

Job: **Word and Action**

his table, and all his sons', also his servants'
tables were unfailingly
bountiful – and I believe him),
then was he something like a spring-fed brook
irrigating the places that would be
too dry for growing, otherwise;
and did that leave him, like
the other wealthy ones
around – and with the help of
sons and servants –
thriving by giving, able
increasingly to raise more crops?

That would have been a
government by the richest, then,
who were to be rewarded
for having done the right thing
always.

The book of Job is no 'Utopia' though.

Events

No seeds of the disasters
that struck were in
the having done it well
surely.
       In one night
everything was wiped out.
Pain and revulsion and
indignities
only, remained.

Job: **Word and Action**

The Reviewer Speculates

Was there a jaundiced eye watching and
hoping perfection somehow would be marred?
Perhaps the followers of his
example, kindly citizens, might
have been inclined, later, to speculate
about some flaw in him
that brought him down.

But they were friends.
They waited
for days for some
evidence, first.

The Issue

A conviction was at stake for
Job – and for his friends.
Job felt it keenly and
for them it mattered too:
to affirm the fairness of
the ethical order. Perhaps they also
felt an obligation to
blame someone – yes, blame Job.
He and his situation
would not fit, otherwise.

Their rock-solid convictions
steadied them in the rough
sea of their friend's
grief, magnificent courage, and
refusal to despair.

Job: **Word and Action**

His struggle to take it, and
to take it in, they did
recognize – but not the
appalling loneliness.

He listened – for
one word to break
in upon the core of his
desolation. Their
speaking only defined
a special doom he stoutly
denied himself
i.e. that he was quite
alone in a
though baffling and beautiful
yet meaninglessly devastating
homeless wilderness.

The Reviewer Interpolates

Your reviewer had expected
something quite different in the
working out of the story.
Visitors spent days counselling
contrition as a therapy,
or equanimity (from
someone *in extremis!*). Distance
lends its own perspective.

Surely God would come and
console His child.
After all, it was Job

Job: **Word and Action**

nonetheless kept his grip
who, in the first shock,
firm on one reality:
the One with all
power was in the end the
only trustworthy one.

He was not consoled.

Was Job being honoured then
for enduring?

Was it that either comfort or
compensation would have seemed …
patronizing?

In any case it only
made sense – read it yourself and
see what you think –
this way, for me, right now:

Wrath Is Felt from Its Source

What was pushing the Other
past patience?
>   Of course there is no parallel
>   anywhere.
>   But a person can
>   remember standing at a bedside
>   ineffectually and
>   seeing somebody in dire distress,
>   who is isolated by it

Job: Word and Action

and fights off isolation, and
gropes for vital contact.
The person keeping vigil
trembles within, knowing
no means but touch, and voice.
These don't get through.
Words evaporate then.

Soliloquy

There is no way
to open my counsel.
I have been close by
knowing ahead that I would have to choose
powerlessness. No
intervening. And would be
unable to explain –
and all because I
trusted your integrity, Job.

But searing is this
wordlessness.

    He was the One to whom
    Job shouted, whispered, always addressing
    the ultimate question.
    Job was tormented to know
    how it could all make sense.

I knew,
but oh, out of Job's range.

    * * *

Job: **Word and Action**

And so the Lord endured –
His Presence like white sound –
while His child struggled to find foothold
in faith, anticipating
deliverance, when the One
who secures all that holds would heed
and show the way and
finally force his battered
misunderstandings to be gone.

Understanding?

No words but His own
word can be
reliable, or safely used
in speculation.

When He confused their language
at Babel, and the achievements
crumbled, wasn't that
merciful?

> Somebody said
> (I'm quoting) 'There is a
> danger that everything, through being misnamed,
> will be misunderstood,' something like that.

I.e. we go on building on our self-
generated constructs, with a self-
referent valuing. But in a not
self-generated universe.

Job: **Word and Action**

Is our communal language –
dollars and megabytes and so on –
just a few stages past our
Meccano sets?

Hard-won are the words
we need to truly
converse with someone close
and yet mysterious to us.

Impasse

Why can't Job glimpse
the truth of feeling on both sides?
And the sufferer
presses, presses.

> It would be unworthy to
> speak some approximating
> word, not a real answer,
> thus negating your respect
> for the true question. Would you break
> the other's integrity?

No. You plunge him in
terror, and awe:
through indigo ocean currents, among
shelves where coral builds on
coral. To Job's stunned
absorption, teeming creation flashed and,
intricate and monstrous,
its creatures sublimely
untroubled, burned with their being.

Job: **Word and Action**

Job awoke then to a
newly vivid sense of his littleness.

Someone had after all been
listening to him all through
the times he ranted, through his
desperate appeals. Someone had let
the barriers build up
between you, in pure pain.

It came then.
Job was scathed – although
but briefly – by the wrath.

Whatever Job felt when the voice
stormed at him, any reader of this book
is outraged!

> 'Will the one who contends with the Almighty
> correct Him?
> Let him who accuses God
> answer Him!'*
>
> and
> 'Would you discredit My justice
> Would you condemn Me to justify yourself?'†

---

* 40: 1

† 40: 8

Restive Interlude

Did you too, reader,
have to put down the book
to let your seething settle?

E.g. did you too
ask, Was Job wrong
to cry out,
>'If I have sinned
>how do I injure Thee,
>Thou Watcher of the
>hearts of men?'*

>or, 'I call for help but
>Thou dost not answer. I stand up
>to plead, but Thou
>sittest aloof'?†

And then Job listened

even through that storm, intent,
he listened.

The Brief Words of Anger, Over

>That part breaks off. Magenta
>clouds boil away and blanch.

---

* 7: 20

† 30: 20

Job: **Word and Action**

The thunderer abruptly, but
wholly encompasses His man:
plunges him through
night's plotted skies; then floundering
light-flooded skies during a March gale;
vast unvisited snowfields, and
Galapagos's coast.

Then, after those
avalanching wonders,
every creature's every detail was revealed,
a centre of this Other's
acute awareness. Equally.
Prairie crocus or coyote or
seas braiding around Leviathan.

By then Job knew
what it is to be broken and
to be overwhelmed in his littleness by
power, and the glory.

Finis

It ends up not to be
a biography.
Another Presence turns out to be
dominant – yet without Job's
dwindling.
The other is beyond any biographer.
When He speaks for Himself
word and action are all but identical.

When were they not
identical?

Job: **Word and Action**

Concrete and Wild Carrot

Pacing the Turn of the Year

A sudden season
has changed our world.
Everybody is out
to see, or bask, or
with their kind to exuberate.

Everything is new.

Trees that were only sticks
into the overcast
yesterday, are
soft and full of catkins
like newly shampooed children being
readied for the party.

Slender young saplings
shine, all the tender leaves
distinct, notes of music
atremble for a chance musician
strolling by to hear and
play – for everybody, on bikes
or park benches or
wandering along
  the way
  the city buses, dazed,
  wended their way anywhere
  on the odd quiet morning
  the European war
  was somehow ended; nobody
  felt like cavorting, singing,
  dancing, as their parents, 1918,
  in November, had.

A muted celebration
this sudden season.
All but the oak.

Rusty tatters left from far-off August's
      leafy towers and gables,
      in deeps and fullness, the amassing
      in gloom and shadow of
greenness; now
ruined arthritic knobs and wrenched
limbs; next to nothing now
covering his nakedness.

The new is going to last?
These celebrants
toss their curls and
rollerblade past
the question.

It was not posed by the
dour oaks,
stolider even than
      the firs, their shabby
      winter wear refurbished
      at the tips,
standing there woodenly under
scrambling squirrels, a warm bath of
sunshine, thunderstorm,
by turns.

Part of a celebration
is to discover
patience? and how
painful hope can be?

Alone, and mute stands
dark, one huge oak tree.

Present from Ted

It must have been after a
birthday; at Christmastime
daylight hasn't the lambency
I remember as part of
the puzzling present somebody
had given me: a scribbler, empty pages, but
not for scribbling in.
Instead of a pencil box there was
a jelly glass set out, with water, and
a brand-new paintbrush.

The paper was not pretty.
A pencil-point might in an upstroke
accidentally jab a hole in it.

But, painting it –
as I was told to, with only
clear water, 'Behold!'
my whole being sang out, for 'see'
would not have been adequate.

The pictures that emerged
were outlines? I remember
only the paper, and the wonder of it,
and how each page was turning out to be
a different picture.
There were no colours, were there?

In the analogy, there are
glorious colours
and, in some way that lacks
equivalents,
deepening colours, patterns that keep
emerging, always
more to anticipate.

For that there is no other process.

Locked in the picture is
missing the quality of the analogy of
morning light
and the delighted holder of the paintbrush
and who gave him the book, and where he found it.

Towards the Next Change

Leaf on the shrub
let the flow
along the corridors of a
breathing stem
ease to a trickle.

      THE SHRUB: Look for
      no energy now. You're letting in
      the cold!
      My stiffened fingers are
      icy.

            The leaf
sighs and separates itself and
wavers away.

Prairie Poem

For George Grant*

To go from whitewater rivers' valleys or
from the escarpment to
live on the Saskatchewan prairie is
choosing to find out that
space calls, to a reshaping
of person. This is above and
beyond the going to, the choosing.

Reading in the open world of
this writer's geography of
ideas is to look, staggered and
overwhelmed by the
ideas, almost lost in the
panorama of
the living, long dead, to him
present as friends, each lifted face
featured for horizons. For
holding close an everywhere of sky.

---

* George Grant (1918–1988) worked in Adult Education, then after study abroad he became a university teacher, latterly at Dalhousie. He wrote *Philosophy in the Mass Age, Lament for a Nation, Technology and Justice,* etc. etc.

We became friends in Toronto, when George came to recuperate from TB, after duties during the London Blitz. His courage in wartime England as a pacifist was impressive. Later, when studies and teaching took him to other cities, his articles and books kept me in touch. Two writers central to me, Dostoyevsky and Jacques Ellul, cropped up in George's writings. We met again in his York University–McMaster period, when his rambunctious but principled consistency delighted me. George worked under a sky that kept opening out.

The land, the books, can never
swallow you, nor even the
furry spring crocus here – however
small, at vanishing points.

Dividing Goods

They say it's wrong to
push a parable.
Figures of speech are still
themselves responsible for
their tendrils – though these stray.
Words have their life too, won't
compact into a theorem.

Take the story of the Prodigal Son:
an invisible third son is not mentioned,
yet he had it all
had prized it all
wanted all of it
for all so
had himself to leave
it, all.
But this one is the only
visible one. He
tells the family's story,
a simple tale but
somehow unresolved so that
its tendrils cling timelessly.

Through his eyes we see
pathos in their wanting something else.

Fool's gold restores
a starveling's taste for
a healthy meal of bread, at home;

                      or, (the older brother)
wanting something –
because deserving more than
this dogged servitude?

(Yet from the outset
the 'mine', the 'portion that is mine'
had to be less than all.)

All those were
dear to the one who
owns and gives and
loves on.

Ramsden

Let's go to the park where
the dogs and children
cluster and circle and run
under the sombre old trees – they are
hanging on to their swarthing
leaves – while the young
medallioned trees in the early
sun are dancing
among them.
The knapsacked students too
hurtle, always too late, focused
on there, blindingly
swerving out of the now and
here where children and dogs
and a few rather shabby, slow
old ones, straying, move
across the owners, standing with
loose leashes, intent on 'their day'.
The benched but sleepless
mothers and nannies, watching,
are quieted here, warmed and fed
by the good old trees and
the shining little ones.

Balancing Out

He smells of – what?
It's like wet coal-dust.
He came very late:
tangled brown hair, his face
streaked, and bleary;
no gloves, but (Merry
Christmas) from a mission, twice
blest – a good warm coat
that could go anywhere – and had!
now puckered, snagged, hem spread
from sleeping out, and ripped
around one leather elbow,
and buttoned crooked. There were no
other buttons now. He slept
there in his pew.

The giver of his topcoat eerily
watched, her widow's desolation clearly
inconsolable now
(a pang – like joy!),
to see what she had seen
on a fine and steady man
made come full circle on this ruined fellow.

Still, he had his coat,
and she, the echoing years.

The Crux

        Ever see somebody hit bedrock
            too messed up to
              say so too
    hopeless a mess to get his chin
      far enough off the ground to
           even give in?
              deadbeat?

    Know what that's like yourself?

Now can you credit
anyone figuring he had to
steer his fair steady days and nights
deliberately
to some as yet (I'm guessing)
point of light beyond that
abysmal (other people's) living
end?
right down, past, the dead end
to the worst? There wasn't
a 'Lamb of God' for the
then lamb the wolf had torn.
But   there   gleamed
the point.

    Ever see a child in his
    highchair twisting with the
    urgency of now, not knowing how
    or what, only the
    pangs, the poignancy
    of *Don't you see*
    that I need everything
    right now?

He hears help coming.
Hope stills the moment.
Eagerness drums with heels and spoon
in a blissful lurch
towards all tomorrow.

The one the radiance touched
does see
and smile there, in that kitchen.
The point.

Ambivalence

When the shutters are down
the outside work is pleasanter
even when fingers out of the mitts
go numb on the hammer;
the boathouse whispered with
ice-splinters and slush when I fetched the ladder.
We'll have to deal with the chimney
before we can warm the place up
inside, and then the cleaning out and sweeping up
will be dirty jobs before it's safe
to light the kindling, inside.

      After the shutters are up
      let's build a fire
      out here: there's wood
      under the cottage; we can
      open the thermos and eat our lunch
      before we tackle the rest?
      It's pleasurable outside.

Being inside will be good when we're
in and out all the time. It can be cosy
when rain is drumming the roof – but that
fireplace sometimes smokes.
In mid-July
it's stifling under the shingles
even after a midnight swim.
On such a night it is pleasanter
under the stars, outside.

      We've never been here when it's
      outside only wherever you might
      need to be to do
      whatever needed doing –
      after the local wood-and-ice fellow who

helps us has cleared the roof from a heavy snow
and left again.
Then   would it   still   be
better   outside   alone, only   outside?

Relating

Are you a young ant or
a small one?
diligently bent for
somewhere, at any rate.
                        And do you wonder
about your place under the huge
invisibly starry sky
this July morning –
                    as I do mine?

The being of an ant
must mark itself,
an alive being, intricately
impelled to run along like that, at least –
with more segmented strange
awarenesses, beyond
this other living creature's grasp.

Many speak languages
I've never learned.
Is your being one
pictograph, seed of a
word, the gateway to
a language nobody speaks?
So none can read this
unsegmented, unsmall,
shared reality.

The radii of power
are focused down and in
on you and me over our
warped little shadows; they
adjust, this midday instant, to
us, moving.

I greet you on your way.
You greet me too, departing?

Responses

No brilliant sun as earlier when beside the
railing (it had seemed
almost possible for the shadow of me
to ride away on the
shadow of the parked bicycle).

No wind.

These listening leaves
quiet me who am all
eyes; even the dangling
leaves on the young trees listen.
I lean my hand
on the rough bark of the
deepest. It's scarcely cupped
around the ageless ample girth.
My forces gather up like an
athlete's alertness. I am straining to ... hear?

With me, it's tenseness,
apprehension, or
anticipation. But the listening
leaves are easy with it.

Reluctantly, I
move on.

Audrey: A Posthumous Portrait

He moste needs walke in woode
that may not walke in towne.
   – *The Tale of Gamelyn*

Brisk, between musings in
the enchanted forests which
she knows exist for the dead-eyed
lords of the hunt, but whom
she indulges anyway and
for her own purposes –

      out for the hunted there
      not to protect but to continue to
      witness that they all have a chance
                      anyhow.

Has its magnificence – even,
at random, magnanimity.

Does not however
quite fail to preclude
the dreamer in the wood
feeling the hounds' breath on her
bare calves, before the
green chaos of the forest lofts
(is it by now rainforest?)
becomes new cover.

Remembers that
sustenance is from the forest floor.
Windswept up there, then
briskly, though not unaware of
perils, crackling, thuds
all the way down again.
On into town, who may not walk
      in town.

Reversing a Crater

A scrawny old old man
(scarred, bowed down, hounded by
uniformed officials and
safe people afraid to meet his eye)
(was he possibly
a fugitive? certainly in seclusion he
sometimes nonetheless
had friends who came with food
and hoped to hear him rise and toast the king!)

that old old man
wrote me a letter.
How it found its way though
from the last-ditch,
vigilant custody,
and by how many hands,
I cannot grasp. And yet it
has found its way, long afterwards,
to this unlikely megalopolis.

Now I am also aged
in as peculiar a community
as his there must have been.

More than my eighty years had
wracked his bones.
Yet he writes
forceful and drastic words with
the clarity of sealight over high
sheltering shores.

> *Suppose that chunk, that crater-gouging*
> *comet collides with us,*
> *will you say then – with him in his extremity –*

*'The tide of joy, never at ebb, still
surges through us too towards
new coasts, a new completedness'?*

What he said, so say I.

Third Hand, First Hand

The whispers Thomas heard
walled him in with thought,
heartsick, tormented, not
open to silly words.

Flesh to dead body. Then how
alive – and walking, here?
(He faced the brute facts more
than the ten others. He knew.)

Blind in his mirrory grief,
stony, he came to them. And
they heard 'Stretch out your hand....'
Thomas abandoned proof.

They saw because they wanted to?
They all half-doubted when
He asked for fish and honeycomb,
took it, and ate it too.

        It was the doctor later who
        said it had been so.

Notes from Dr Carson's Exposition of I John 5*

                      He takes us into
                      Him-[selfless]-self
                      for saving from
                      what dazed and distracts us
                      as each, preoccupied
                      and swarming lonelily
                      is out for his own for one
                      already fading day.

Why?
Is it the way to
                pure
        delight?
(The very opposite
of what we thought?
                    or not,
we think, fitting for us
as we, ourselves, not His self
would trust)?

---

* Donald A. Carson is a Canadian theologian, presently Research Professor of New Testament, Trinity Evangelical Divinity School, Deerfield, Illinois. This poem refers to a sermon he gave in Toronto.

He Was There
He Was Here

A whiskered mask was all I saw
in the milkers' twilight hour
of the glimmery ghost of Fortinbras
not in Denmark, but here.
Wings creaked, deep before daybreak
and flapped, bird-necks astretch,
out beyond sight in the ghoul-light
(straw-smell, wet armour-brass).

The whiskery glint was gone.
Nobody passed by the smoking glass
of the lost lake either, that morn.

Where he had gone, whom he had seen,
indeed what he might have wanted,
invisibly wired the hours between
wharf and the usual noon canteen,
but it made both disjointed.

As the day wears on, those shinbone greaves
and that bale-bright glaring no one believes,
nor the milkwarm farm he haunted.

Remembering Gordon G. Nanos

Visual memory:
A narrow, uninsistently
dapper 'senior',
felt hat, casual jacket
unassertive,
quietly walking, listening
(usually the companion
was the same lady);

this Residence
has its own Armistice Day
Service: Nanos (air force),
with one (army) major, two
engineering corps men
several nurses etc.,
in the front row, all – old. All standing,
painfully or not,
rigidly upright for
the national anthem.

At a Families' Day
picnic pool
in some hostess's
grassy back yard. Most adults
trying not to slump
in shiny patio furniture
observed, smiling to see
splashers and little dancers in the sun.

Nanos? He'd slipped away;
nobody had noticed
his little satchel.
The costume, when he appeared!!

In swimsuits, dripping still, gathered
the children, all aglow,
enchanted by his nods and capers
marvelling at his magic.

Nanos is gone
after four-score years. I see
a clown's death has
a spacious dignity.

Other Oceans

1. On

When the convulsive earth
arched under the sea
its craggy ribs were
blurted out where reefs had been
into the golden warmth for a
fraction of a second of the one
day that's a thousand years.
In the same breath, on what was risen up
swarms of wee morsels mightier than
seafoam, rockface, under weather
brought what had emerged to be
grasses of the field
breathing that sun-washed sky.
On the face of the earth
trees and tiny Arctic flowers
face upwards; animals
with velvet paws, or hoofs,
all seem to look away towards the
falling-away edge of the earth.
My face, among these others,
ours, are not as though
among these others.

2. Within

Studies by night. By day
blinks at the intricate
script of the world. A levelling
fuzzy peach morning-light
blurs what it would
make plain. Not
soundlessly. Whirrings.

Faint sighs. Intrudes
the throb of self selecting self
out of what was suggestive of a
singing part. Unravels
some syllables of the music, in
withdrawing again.
Waits. Cannot not be expressed
but in some foreign idiom
that seems fitting although
unspoken.
    Waits
unscrolling somewhat
lopsidedly from
the effort of withholding
intrusion. Tense. Welcomes
the night's return, and sleep.

3. Under

A morning triangle of shadow
divides this field. On three
sides the building bulks.
A glimmering mesh of some
impenetrable composite substance
seals in the fourth. The grass-blades
are metal tongues, so hinged
that two or three persons, let out
under the pitiless sky
for daily exercise,
can shuffle through it,
or wade, or clatter and kick
as competency or their residual
savagery permits.

These little metal grass-blades
are mathematically precise
like tree-trunks in a forested
field in France.

Somewhere the warden
sits, nettled by the clicking
of footsteps in the field,
or yard.

People outside
steel themselves to resist
any convulsive surge to storm
this new Bastille.
Nobody seems to know

why some are in there, some,

less contained, out here.
Only a scattering
at any one time stand, and then
move on across their own
shadows in the wide courtyard.

Remember, even food and drink
turned into metal. Then it was gold,
under a Midas touch that menaces
and unmakes
heroes and revolutionaries.

People's singular sense of things
is everywhere too private
(or too prearranged)
for any foreseeable action but
perseverance only.

The skies will ember into the
deep darkness of another
night, and sleep –
that chrysalis of waking.

4. When

'O God, God of all flesh …,'*

supreme artist, originator
of all designs, who sees:
for us the entering in
is long deferred, while
  'praise' in our tongue
  is merged with 'price' –
  (could we go back to 'laud', or
  that other word from
  'loben',
  instead?)
Far off is that horizon
of calm and contained
joy that is wholly
unselfconscious, simple,
lovely. Where is the holy
vanishing point
where life began and daily may
bring us alive
again? Is this
being alive?
The far-off isn't, and is all
that is.

---

* The cry of Moses and Aaron over Korah *et al.*

5. Where

Hard-edged day time does
usually recur. Same glare,
same silent
engrossing shadow.
The park is lifting up
bare branches in bouquets.
One, shafted by the sun, offers its small
flambeau. Wires
tangle underfoot and would entangle.
This place seems unfrequented.
But specks like filings
move (tilted, trickling?) (alive!)
on a dry root.
Oak trees rustle
for long months, driving
their roots down still.

6. Out

Though helpless, here,
whoever cried out and was heard
in darkness, in quietness,
is charged:
stand; wait here,
for some lame stumbler, for
random young shufflers,
         for skyfall.

Stand, day in, day out,
readied for day upon day.

* * *

The frozen sheets
after we fetched them in
crackled as we folded them
for propping, splayed
out on the wooden racks
in the back kitchen.
Icy sunlight gleamed
on the waxed kitchen floor.
Down went a pair of brooms
criss-cross.
'This is the sword dance!'
and Katie showed me,
leaping and flashing. Note
this was not bonny Sco'land, it was
a lowering prairie 2 p.m. and at a
scourging forty below!

　　　* * *

At first light, on a
certain day, someone appeared, bearing
a floor-piece on his shoulders.
Its underside was flat; the other side
had wooden cleats between the wooden slats.
When he laid it level, and inside there,
you saw its wood was sun-bleached.

Nobody saw how he got in!

The old hinged metal tongues that were the
grass-blades were on a level other than
where he now steadily walked
towards the little exit-entrance doorway to
the exercise yard or punishment area.

We numbly witnessed as
a hissing skirt of fire swept
under and around
him and his platform. An air hose
soon restored the metal grass.
The solitary, once again
emerged to pace as every clicking day
they did.

Among the young, some spoke
secretly hoping to turn
their hero's grisly defeat into some
concerted attempt,
maybe more
influential and more daunting, to
unearth the incarcerator of
so many, singly – and
then to get word back, to stir up
recruits, to reconnoitre
deeper into the
secret power and the source of power.

Among the older, worn by day
upon hypnotic day,
the hope was hope for stamina
not for success, and for
courage for those more able.

'O God, God of all flesh!'

Behold the immured, the lost champion,
the dangerously young,
and us who merely persevere
along the borders of
the always unthinkable!

7. After

Post-modern:

i.e. those who (he said)
in honesty of heart
deny any eternal verities; being
searchers for plausible
truth, they humbly
substitute for the old symbols,
what they affirm as
'the logocentric'.

You know their thoughtful
responsible faces, their
capacity for goodness, their
willingness to show
good will.
They shoulder only their part of the
burden of living as a
matter of course.

Who can help warmly
appreciating such people
among us, leaders of thought,
careful, and when necessary, bold
in action?

How different it would be, today, to
'take up your cross and follow Me', to
'take My yoke upon you, learn....'
Take both? Take what's to hand? Find
one follows the other? or
find the same bewildering burden?

It makes no sense today
to talk this way, nor did
in A.D. 30, thereabouts.
No, but once heard it condenses
somehow. Cautions. Compels – can
flood a person, earth and sea and sky – all that
originated in a like
mystery (all who will die from
this reasonable lifetime we have known) –
with one
overwhelming focus,
for what remains of your
lifetime's doings and responsibilities,
held by a steadying pulse.

And whether some finally
together break out till
the stars fall, or
a sudden global change
freezes inhabitants' pulses

>	one artist who, in one
>	impulse once called out, from surging
>	waters and fires and molten
>	rock
>	our earth, our little lives,
>
>	maintains, Himself, the
>	no longer appearing
>	structures.

The Whole Story

Behind that stone before
it was rolled away
a corpse lay.
There lay all I deplore:
fear, truculence – much more
that to any other I need not say.
But behind that stone I must be sure
of deadness, to allay
self-doubt, i.e. so nearly to ignore
the love and sacrifice for our
release; to nearly stray
back into the old
pursuit of virtue.

Once it is clear
it was a corpse that day,
then, then, we know the glory
of the clean place, the floor
of rock, those linens, know the hour
of His inexplicable 'Peace'; the pour
– after He went away –
of wonder, readiness, simplicity,
given.

Cycle of Community

Mid-morning paraffin film over the
dayshine has
incidentally opened the ear
to little clanks and whirrs
out there, the hum
of a world going on,
untroubled by the silent witness, sky.
We here are silent. Yet being
drawn into, with, each
creature, each machine-work
thump, each step, faraway bark,
buzz, whine, rustle, etc.
goes to give our city
a voice, dampered by distance;
serves, through outer
windless openness of skywash, to
open a bud of tremulous hearing.

Full day will blare away
later. Then –
walk (an even pace) where cars, trucks, a
cement-mixer, teenagers out of school,
and a tied puppy keening
outside the grocer's,
provide a mix the studios would
take pride in.
Go steadily for your sake and
the others' on the sidewalk
burrowing by. And keep your face
like anyone's, in
pedestrious preoccupation –
although
you'll have to part your lips
a little, to play in.

First, test the pitch of the
prevailing din
(humming), then (still with no
perceptible opening of the mouth)
intone on the same tone-level
with all the enveloping street-sound.
Louder. As loudly as you can!
Nobody hears a thing,
                          even yourself!
Otherwise surely someone would
give that quick glance of
furtive avoidance that flicks
some flushed and angrily
gesturing man you may
hear shouting along
anywhere about town. He chooses
to stray apart from the
condemnable crazy world.

Surprisingly, evening, after the hours
of sharp light, closes in
overcast. Our thunderous busynesses
shift into calmer surge and flow.
Before dark (sky and windows
contemplating emptiness) we half-
hear the foghorn and remember
the lake, and night.

Seriously?

Chaos means ... 'gape'!
                                       It does?
Look up the derivation!
'Utter confusion' is just
dragged in by connotation
with the dreaded Abyss.
'Old night'[*] is now all wizened.
The new cosmography says
maybe even the bottomless isn't!

Murky and ennui-ridden
is the malodorous midden
earth has become. But it soon will be gone
down – in a 'yawn'!

---

[*] Milton's phrase.

Dead Ends

The dead end that I dreaded
confronts me in this
true statement!

It's apt, manageable, but
valid only in its locked cabinet.
There's no finality out here: a sphere
too vast, too growthful, too
mischievous; subject as well
to swellings, violent
combustion, whizzings off
along the light-years.

There's too much
of us for us to know.
But closing heart, and ear
is a terminus I
fear, too.
        We slam
into it, often, though knowing is a peril
almost as terrible as
never being sure
where
the dead end will
appear.

Prospecting

There is a node. There, one day,
all ways will
swiftly converge.

> Evening's, or morning-
> star glimmers from dear old –
> too old now – burlap earth-skies.

> Behold the abandoned
> once historied
> home of us people.

Our present
orbital rush singles out some
veering.
Plumblines occur.

> (Abandoned? no,
> not yet quite smouldered out within
> a few of us.)

All waves
(once ear and eye and intuition's
and science's) wash into
symphonic silence.

Time, too.

For at the node
all energies become
that unrewarded effortless and
ruthless kindness,
Person.

Lament for Byways

The harrowed city
swirls with grit;
it's thundery
with chutes emitting
shards, broken stone
from in behind
brickwork going, gone
to dust within.
New little canopies
appear. Wooden partitions
shield the passerby
from inward operations
(something else under the wrecker,
shovel, and scoop …). Through spy-
holed fences, we inspect
the backs of streets we knew
before.

                Some starts should not be
                stopped at a dead end.
                This habitual short-cut ought to
                open on my old friend
                the boarded-up, blue, disused
                warehouse, well known to me.
                Here where it stood is – just a
                pavement! and empty sky!

With the old short-cut in mind
will we bear with it, white and flat?
Somehow the cars keep blinding
the last few alleys we had.

These handsome new high-rises
help us to overlook
throbbing cement-truck noises
and gritty slime underfoot.

Yesterday's old blue eyesore is
now a new tidied-up site,

but, my city, it's still in your lanes and mews
that your heart beats.

Rising Dust

The physiologist says I am well over
half water.
I feel, look, solid; am
though leaky firm.
Yet I am composed
largely of water.
How the composer turned us out
this way, even the learned few do not
explain. That's life.

And we're in need of
more water, over and over, repeatedly
thirsty, and unclean.

The body of this earth
has water under it and
over, from
where the long winds sough
tirelessly over water, or shriek around
curved distances of ice.

Sky and earth invisibly
breathe skyfuls of
water, visible when it
finds its own level.

Even in me?
Kin to waterfalls
and glacial lakes and sloughs
and all that flows and surges,
yet I go steadily,
or without distillation climb at will
(until a dissolution
nobody anticipates).

I'm something else besides.
The biochemist does not
concern himself with this.
It too seems substance,
a vital bond threaded on an
as-if loom out there.
The strand within
thrums and shudders and twists.
It cleaves to this
colour or texture and
singles out to a rhythm
almost its own, again,
anticipating design.

But never any of us
physiologist or fisherman
or I
quite makes sense of it. We
find our own level

as prairie, auburn or
snow-streaming, sounds forever
the almost limitless.

Two

Trees breathe for any
who breathe to live.

      Stone makes every thing
      more what it is:
      sun-hot,

late November bare,
cold in an early April morning;

    age in being
    always.

Leading Questions

Walking naked in Eden, they
lived always in the light
of the holy. Drawn to disobey
they awoke to shame – and God-

like comprehension of pain,
of broken as well as good.
(What would *our* choice have been
if we had understood?)

And what was the shame about?
And why did He need, then,
to 'clothe the lilies …', who night-
ly met those unclad in Eden?

Had nakedness not meant freedom?
At evening, now forsaken
by our choice, was that to Him
as since to us, heartbreaking?

Yet He taught the Jews to weave
rich fabrics for the abode
He would live in, or above
in fire or (covering) cloud,

and long since He has promised to prepare
for us the robe He hopes His guests that Day will wear.

Uncircular

The entombment of all that wrath
bespeaks the stench of a
fragmenting into
finality.
To me, this matters.
I anchor there as to a lifeline,

      * * *

there where
what other self-bound persons
had wrapped and lovingly
laid, a total
loss for all, for all
was found in purity, among his friends
changed, but the same time opening
everything on earth to the
power that lifted him.

No wonder Paul cried out,
'I count all loss …' – above all, loss.

      * * *

Among us, Jesus found
encrusted words and structures;
he washed and brushed them clean
and out of the intractability
of history learned by rote
stepped, in simplicity the exemplar,

into the prairies of
dutiful days, each with the taste
of moving slowly towards … without
the horizon coming any closer.

His are the evenings of a
king in a cave kept wakeful by
deftly deciphering the
poems he found written in his heart.

When most of his people trailed
about in moulting plumage –
aping, through fear and envy,
those not themselves –
he brokenheartedly
tried to put heart in them
again, or rouse them to the dread, in time,
that dragged them down
into sensibility.

In the besieged city
he moved among the panic-crazed;
and where skin-and-bone
cannibals crept or
by the walls, rocked against the rock
like a cribbed infant.
Once for a time
all of them were
strangers far from home.
They knew the wreckage to be
faced and put together somehow
on their return some day.

Once again there, Jesus too found
words twisted, rubble about, and
again he swept and tended them
gently, almost smiling
when some who so cherished
the traditional that they urged
stains, gritty particles, dust

must be left, too, untouched.
His words flowed from a
clear wellspring always till now
a little tainted by the
hand that cupped to drink, or the
crafted ladle.

Why was this one then
dragged off and left abandoned to
indifferent cruelty once, with no
home left, anywhere?

              * * *

Entombment, however, is
new in all history.
What it is for.

The Endangerer

Swept in among the wave-suds,
moved gently out, and in,
flotsam, he lay, a log
to any shorewalker.
And one approached. He always came
at sundown.

Alive still? Yes!
The rescue crew he brought
churned up the shore, so that the slant sun
made a lengthening shadow behind
every clump, a dot at every grain.

Today, erect, the stranger
strolls past his unremembered
couch among the
shell-chips and weedy runnels.

And there before him, prone,
the swelling waters brim,
benign, bemusing:
'This watery world is flat, and every wavelet
is a homecoming from the bourne.'

It had taken a further journey for the
convalescent to
frame – and paint out – the lie.

To Wilfred Cantwell Smith*

When asked, What is an intellectual? he said: 'An intellectual is a participant in his own society, listening to people. That kind of truth cannot be put anywhere by us, not in words, never put in its place. The human mind can apprehend, not comprehend.'

Our native language shapes us, does it not
even as it shapes itself upon the page?
The languages you've learned, in life and college,
carve and emboss characters in your thought?

> Hebrew's ornate iron, its quirks around the line
> (vocal or consonant) in you have wrought
> the odd intransigent openness – and untaught
> much we grew up to mimic – or disdain.

---

* Wilfred Cantwell Smith (1916–1999) was introduced to Canadian readers in 1962 by the published CBC series *The Faith of Other Men*. His last two books, in 1998, are *Patterns of Faith Around the World* and *Faith and Belief*. Reference works call him an 'Islamicist' – see his *On Understanding Islam*, 1984. He taught at McGill, Dalhousie and, for the last years, as Professor of Comparative Religion at Harvard.

In failing health, he and his wife moved to the seniors' residence where I live. The in-house paper delegated me to interview him simply as a new resident. The Smiths' friendly unassuming welcome made it easy, although I was awed to learn that Wilfred spoke Urdu, Arabic and many European languages, and his wife (a surgeon who practised in India before Partition) spoke Punjabi and some oriental languages as well. Until their health forced a move to nursing care, I had the joy of reading aloud (his sight was increasingly poor) many an afternoon, with breaks for conversation. The epigraph records one comment he made in passing!

Myopic, skeptical, sometimes distraught,
slowly your readers see ourselves as foreign,
trotting for safety through our little warren
of walled ways. Now, perilously, we're out

in a big world of foreigners, finding that they are not!
Ink on white paper keeps informing those
who learn, to listen long, until there glows
within the friendly signs of being understood.

    Urdu's visual/inner shapes I've not
    seen on the page to see in you. I know
    Persian and Arabic's fluid music though
    (to the eye); which to your nature also brought

a spare poetry. Such surprises dot
and wink away through universal
(meticulously measurable)
spaces, and what's been sought
within shines there, articulate, through the night.

Four Words: A Gloss on I Cor. 14: 6

Revealed
The other has confronted,
touched on the quick, borne with through
awful combative silence – almost
inaction – until knowing one is
known, now.

Knowing
One is the observer of,
made participant in,
momentarily
caught, stilled;
listens with every fibre;
and to the swiftly far away
vanishing, an unpursuer
humbled.

Prophecy
Words are
imparted, able to calm,
quick to wrestle – and best;
they map a long long travelling
beyond experience even.

Teaching
Small exaltations of spirit demand
groundedness. Now too long
past dawn it's time to get down to
listening, learn to talk too
without interference from
yourself, doing what's been
given to be done.

On a Maundy Thursday Walk

The Creator was
walking by the sea, the
Holy Book says. Finely tuned
senses – flooded with
intense awareness – tested
a clear serene constancy.

Who can imagine it, sullied
as our senses are? Faulty as are even our
most excellent makings?

The perfection of
created Being, in the perfect
morning was born from the walker-by-the-sea's
imagination. At a word –
the hot smell of sunned rock, of
the sea, the sea, the sound of lapping, bird calls,
the sifting sponginess of sand
under the sandals, delicate
April light – all, at a word
had become this almost-
overwhelming loveliness.

Surely the exultation –
the Artist
Himself immersed in
His work, finding it flawless –
intensified the so soon
leaving (lifted out of
mortal life for good
forever).

That too eludes
us who disbelieve that we
also shall say goodbye to
trees and cherished friends and
sunsets and crunching snow
to travel off
into a solo death.

How much more, that
(suffering this
creation to go under
its Maker, and us all)
He, the Father of love, should stake it all
on a sufficient
indeed on an essential
pivot.

In Our 'Little Nests'

To freely write or say
what may give offence
is finding one's not free
or – was, at great expense.

Tut-tuttery today
fits politics. The ones
who judged censoriously
in opposition once

when their party prevails
in power, discover why
solutions will entail
the problems they decry.

One set on sensibly
pricking ballooning notions
before they ride too high
flattens some fond illusions.

After the hullabaloo
what will be assessed?
Whose thinking will come through
as troublesome – at best?

        * * *

Meaning no harm is nice since

it's seeing no harm really.
Who cares? It provides licence
to speak out freely.

Contextualizing, *or* Neither Here Nor There

To 'hate those who hate You' –
or you –
(rather than those who may be
    out-and-out down on me)
seems a moral necessity
encompassed in
    'loving our enemies'.

                    Out here
there's an unconscious undertone
of fond contempt, at best,
when anyone adverts to what
once mattered so much
to other shapers of
style, in opinion. Here
cuttings from the hothouses
(where yesterday's flowers of the field are
coaxed to limp survival)
are cherished as new rank
growth, for general benefit out here
– without embarrassment
of wormy soil, or festering, or
composting at the end perhaps.

                    Inside
there comes sick longing to be out from under
shelter in the bald day,
even to wither there.
                    Out here
with hate, loving, it can too soon
begin to seem
cool, that 'shadow of turning'.

                        Inside
it's harder still to sidestep
minimal, chilling compromises –
too little respecting, or
too defensive about our
amazing range of individualities
under the one rubric that matters.

Alternative to Riots But All Citizens Must Play

To myself everywhere:
Cry out, 'Break!' Break
all our securities, and break out!
Explore only the ranges
beyond our mastering. Take on
the inexorable demands made by
a norm of unpremeditated excellence!

* * *

Forget the elegant speeches,
the unbreakable delicacy
or cello resonance of
'art'. Forget
faceless, imperial (worldwide)
governance and its shimmery
statistical sheen. Why,
even the memory traces of
classical Greece's music are
long forgotten. (The Empire then was Rome's.)

Our own skills and
achievements are imprisoned by
managed relationships
no one can manage, quite.
Money we used to see,
in metal baubles, jig along the wires.

(Back when the new technology
was electricity,
the first department stores were
festooned with maypole-radiating wires.
The dancers' ends came down to
clerks parcelling purchases.
The money offered and the invoices
were stuffed in metal baubles and sent off

jigging up the wires
to the store's one
change-maker, stamper of receipts,
set apart up on a
mezzanine level, caged
but always in plain view.)

Money is no longer
visible. Now
it vaporizes and disperses somehow
and settles over all of us.
We turn into a monstrous
sameness, a jumble
within one skin,
a skin pulled taut
until it hurts
the whole ungeographical
world of us.

Break out! Break from all safe
comprehensive arrangements
never completely comprehended by
controllers or controlled.
Once there were landscapes, features,
rugged outcropping, signatures
bespeaking persons. Now they all melt into
categories, till conglomeration
begins to make categories
a fiction, although still
a soothing one.
Security shackles us in shame and helplessness; the
insecure are bony; they
shuffle past, lean
anywhere, drained clean of
expecting, or of anything

beyond the courage to go on
dully surviving.

Beware of any notion of
safety from having clustered under
some forced, or chosen,
minority. All of them are
self-centred, all a
security that blinds and deafens
exposing flank, and heart
to poisons from within as well.
Where can anyone find
sanctuary, now that
lethal puffs drift
out of a fair sky,
drift down?
Gunshot crackles in the
streets after our sheltering
walls have crumpled.
And still the illustrious ones, the
conference diplomats, the key
negotiators – a unique
minority – are
emperors on parade,
unaware of being not even
clad let alone cloaked.

Some count on the majority
out there, bland in its
openness, our security in
the social swim. But like so many sure
foundations, latterly, this one
seems unsettlingly wobbly.
The animus keeps fading into
passivity. Many that were

supports, happily tolerating
anything – almost – now
lean, to imbalance, straggling off.
Stop them! Disrupt these
almond-eyed visions, spongy with
yearnings, for prophesied
pre-dawn light, this very day.

Nightfall is near.

Break in! Break up
all our so solid structures for the
glory of
nothing to hold on to
but untried air currents,
the crack and ricochet
of impact. Risk
survival! into
some indestructible
transmuted loss. There will begin,
perhaps, a slow
secret, gradual, germinating
in the darkness.

Too Towards Tomorrow:
New Poems

The Fixed in a Flux

From the back seat, barley fields and sky
jolt into: shacks, outbreaks of
garish little gas
stations wherein shine
those cabinets of pop. It's like
a breathing-out relief,
being borne on, to
gaze again out over
unfenced pastureland
in a light that is a
misty blue-spruce colour.

Such a traveller
sees, certainly, and yet
with a kind of non-
seeing. Still the particulars
stand out, accurate
to a roof-slant with
partly fallen chimney
or that tall ditch-top spike
of thistle, odd, in silhouette against
nothing. This non-seeing calls for only
a moving car – or train window.

Freed from responsibility to
everyday eyework, non-seeing
peaceably receives, without withholding
acceptance.

Persons with a point of view say 'I
see,' to one another, but when
drawn through a keyhole of a solitary time,
are simply open
to what, in time, must pass;
all that is seen being there
a now that nonetheless is not
quite here.

Ne Cedere: 'Won't Go Away'

(Written in August, 2001, before 9/11)

You stubbed your toe
that time, on
'necessity'. You
flinched, chose constructs of
your devising, necessarily
contrived by those at hand.
A tower and looming:
security for
you, aloft, within.

You insecure down on the street
flirt with necessity,
choosing for the moment
only. Let sundown be
some brand-new necessity.

And if doom fall on
all, of necessity
because the constructs toppled
on dancers in the street,
boom! And then silence,
rescuers too being done for.

Necessity can comment:
'pressure
without, within.'

Who are you, then, necessity?
A scrawny neck. Squatting
so you're half-hidden.
Just enough hair to
be whipped up in the wind.

Are you our excuse
for 'having to' consume all we
'had to' produce, since we grew
bored with the slow-paced
secluded days of
bare necessities?

Too Towards Tomorrow

Golden meadows of morning, evenings
when the last glister of
birdsong vanishes and
only the nighthawk is
still away out up there in the
gathering dark:

such an – arena! that word is
unnerving. Arena? To
emerge out of the other
earnest contestants would be
good? For what? For whom?
That a fair summer's loveliness
stirs impatience for
showing how knowing
bliss brings, in a darker
place, triumph!

The onslaught when it hits
will be far
other. To survive
one by one will be
owing to somebody else's
eleventh-hour intervention.

Resolute Lament

So far to go.
      Some buds in some
      places, some times
      seal, for safety.

So far so far.
      First light finds
      secrets in its 'white' self.
      Colours stipple the cumulus
      and crest in almost
      kept secret.

Here now and
yet not weary.
      In one day, he
      was not, and then
      Elijah ran like a steer.
      Utterly spent. Having been
      witness of the
      massacre, though he knew
      those smoking ruins ended
      enemies of all pure
      joy in being.

What if
they be friends?
If brothers?
What of
the one good?

So far to go, blinded
by shards.
      By now the mountainous west
      gulps the last light before
      its time.

Nahuatl/*Tomana* (to Swell)

Between here and the window
there bobbled that
tomato-shaped head, its
dent bottle-green stubble,
its face tomato-shiny,
eyes a seed-flat gleam
ominous in its non-com-
municating. I
half-rise, peer back, pretending into
window-glassed night.

Not a word
from either

until, by daylight, one
concession:
'Be who you may
come as you choose until
the slump of greendark
rottenness,
and then, stay out! (under
the window, facing still
away from night).'

Anything beyond this
must be proscriptive.

Cosmosis

Imagine knowing what you have
known about! Startles
the very eyebrow hairs.
Will it open out, on
unknowable deeps, with star-gleam?
Smallens an already
small one here, among this
sun's flock, and on
the marbled and blue one –
us.

Once long ago, before
he could talk, Carl had been put
into the wintry yard in his
snowsuit, to play.
There he'd been
rooted, staring at the
dead starling, fringe of wing
stuck on ice, spiky,
unmoved by the cold that breathed
down from a far cold sky.
Knowing, before he knew
about 'dead', had been
with him down his years.

Nothing explains the known. Nothing
will spare another child one day the
solemn chill.
Eyelashes of first
snowflake on the cheek
although a clue to cherish
remain as inexplicable
as what we know is a
swerve propelling mortal
us, pivoted with our light's

planetary cluster in
place and time around
the vastness beyond.

Walt knew the importance of
the place of abode he kept
maintained, for him and family.
He spent long days however in
board rooms, conference rooms
among charts and reports, and on
frequent flights, always with
home as pivot.

But the day fell –
perhaps he'd heard about the
prospect but discounted it.
His place of abode, for all its
roseate stability,
became – in a few
shuddering moments (only a chance
to escape out to the lawn) –
bottomless, the foundation
crumbs. It was some heretofore
undetected geological fault
maybe, of course
unforeseen. He
knew: unsafety,
uncertainty, a queer
jolt in the identity he'd always
shared with his place of abode.

What might seem
disasters, out
in space, are known about,
that is, predictable

in the far sight of some:
one probable ratcheting up of
ongoingness, out there.
Now it is known.

Slowly, perilously,
interacting is found to be
secured against collisions.
Nonetheless
space remains the isolator
to those who come
to know, here, on this earth.

Early Easter Sunday Morning Radio

    The young voices,
    the students' choirs
    stir wonder. It's

the sting of new day
clear   chill   delicately
touched on the damp
grey-cloth east by a
thin brush, watery colours
faint in: tints run
sidewise and dis-
solve upward in the not yet except
for a breath of, a
far-off heralding of,
sun.

    'Gloria!' they sing,
    'Gloria!'

Why weep, old eyes, when
so suffused with joy?

Three Shore Breakfasts

After a sleepout, after a swim
scalded and buoyant with cold:
fire, and a cookout. A whitethroat's hymn
ripples the mirroring quiet

of morning. This is bodily joy
alive – from a lifetime ago.
Body was caught up in sun and sky.
Far from this evening's snow.

>Some nights out
>are nightshifts. Dull.
>Bone-wearying, but
>all for nothing at all.

>Why go there then?

>The forge we were meant
>to work, was gone
>to the government.

>Families to feed,
>Despair to fight,
>needed a good
>tough slogging night.

How could a breakfast have outweighed that?
Friendliness warming the heart;
warmth for the belly, a share in the food –
and pay packets, coming in late!

Open

Those drawn by light
find it is night they see by,
and shrivel. What outshines
is death.

Some survive, trembling, but then
evaporate –
body and soul and iridescent
fading-out eyes –

yet to be discovered
still standing, shaky
under the constant pour
of light.

Moths around a lamp will see
morning never again
nor even the mild breathing
of sunset.

Night comes. And
goes, in nature;
not, now, at home
nor in its necessary season
at the unvisited pole.

Ex-Communicants

The iron trellis frame, with dots
at their arrhythmic intervals,
black, here and everywhere, recalls
intransigent loyalty of thought.
It marks myopics, or distraught
learners in an alien land.
These have to cling, to understand
the new, to the familiar. Hence
our thinking's mutual intransigence.

To break the cast of thought and travel free
may cost each fourteen years in Araby.

But One Recoiled (Ezekiel 9)

When God determines not to spare
must we not care?

'They threw the boomerang,' He said,
'Their dodges let it strike them dead,
nor will I interfere.'

Some have been marked, who were
uneasy, before.
Their little cross is fair.

One day the One will bear
the one that will deliver
us from the boomerangs we threw – and more!

Because Your Hour Is Dark

Everyone has some clue, enough to
think he knows what it is
now, for you. Your still
banked-on lifelong loyalty
churns in a dark closing-in place inside you.
Look away to 'the way'?
Yes, as exhorted, you do – and contemplate,
wall-eyed, weariness only.

>In John 13, Jesus
>told his men separation
>was his way; they could
>not follow, then. And
>bade them love – without him.

Despair
is different. Is for those
defeated in their desirings;
they've never come to know
this wider, bleaker landscape.
Animals cough here, in the half-light.
Some prowl. You try to hunt down
peace like a prey.

>'Where is he gone?'
>Dimly, following the blank
>wall, they question:
>'Through? he'll be broken....'

To look forward to
only fluttery bed curtains, closed,
one day. And solicitous strangers
helping you collect the last
strands, last link to a dead world.
(You've seen this – down the ward.)

(Not your experience yet, except for
this total aloneness under heaven.)

        'You will be scattered ...,'
        he warned. Then he
        will be left, alone.

So – not alone?

A merest whiff
of other weather somewhere
wafted from where love is forever
in blossom, among orchards also
always laden with fruit.

Ajar

    Solstice: oranges beside a
    jar of pussy willows.
    Opening day ahead for
    rolling your hoop in the wide, wide world.

OR

    A glistening sea spread under
    the teal-blue sky,
    level horizons all around. By
    some eerie miracle
    everything tilted towards the
    edge-of-nothing end.

AND

    Toiling ahead
    through long wet rasping
    grasses in dimness.
    Delicate apricot and lilac tints.
    A hint of the imponderable
    power of glory – thickets, end of
    everything else to be
    faced first.

    The forecasts, all:
    fair weather.

Strolling

In an unfamiliar city
walking vaguely as a visitor
must, to be properly in
a place (not a discrete
bead rolling on an unaccepting surface),
that unexceptional morning
as I walked,
sounds from a few streets over
drew me, a people-gathering murmur.

I followed the trickle of
latecomers magnetized, as I was,
towards the right place
at the right time.

Oh, it made us glad
to see the bright blazers. It was
a parade: small inexpert
bands, the always to be
counted on small boy
trotting along, in time.
The audience was sparse
in any one place, all eyes.

Why did it bring
tears to my eyes and that odd
ache in the throat, as I
turned away to seek again
the anonymity of this
unfamiliar city?

Sad Song

You open your eyes on a lonely light.
Something not there you'd dreamed would be.
Utterly lost from all company you
yield to an absence from long ago
looking for pencil-tracings out on the
waiting wash of the lonely light.

The End Not Yet

See – after the shampoo
the nursery loveliness of a
fair wisp unfurling in sunshine,
small, and astir with
the child's implicit
beauty.

Out west, on that abandoned
farm, the garden
has gone to seed.
Filaments gleam, fronds curl.
No gently fumbling hand
touches, any more. And yet
living is bent on dancing towards
the autumnal lumber room.

A cabin burned alone with its
forest. The cindersmell
is rank. Roots smoulder on: a
tentative curl of smoke is
touched to an auburn arc where
a sunbeam finds it out.

Loveliness anoints
every prong of grief and loneliness
mindlessly, livingly.

Betrayed into Glory (John 13: 32)

Separation was His way.
We could not follow there;
but where we stay, can we obey
and – love? – those in His care?

No. We are unable.
The wall He's passing through
does not show it's feasible,
and He is lost to view.

Has He required
what we can't do?
with not a word
to tell us how?

Is there some wall,
some passing-through
for us, as well?
Absurd! But it is so.

And it is He!
Over, under,
around, away …?
Dimly I wonder:

through? He'll be broken!
And I'll be dead.
No word is spoken.
I forge ahead,

stubborn, to holy ground.
And, there, first, love is found.
The troubled way I went
is what He meant!

'I Wondered As I Wandered'

Before the beginning, before there was any before
or any ever after, only
the unchanging was.
Why, in that unimaginable
counsel chamber, was creation ever
contemplated? Before,
there was quiet, with
dynamics of joy
ever undisturbed, zinging
along at the pace of play, or in
a museful dance, a wrappedness in
continued discovery of the
known person.

Creation would be
other, but like.

That 'like' flashes, instantaneously:
danger!
There they'd be free, but free
to comprehend as well
eye-shine in dark places; 'like', but not with
simultaneous comprehension of
equipoise.

To share is to consent
to sure loss.
A pianissimo threnody is borne
along among the choirs
of thousands upon thousands of
angels. A new
poignancy has been
born. It is
necessary, for hope.

Rafters of forever
will be in place, in time.

Loam

FROM the city's captives who
sense spring, strolling,
breathe the early fresh, or
less congealing, air: a vote of thanks

TO the City Parks Department who
reach out from the high-risen new
city hall, out, to the lowliest
vacant lot or triangle
left over from some city-building planned
in the old affluent days.

The green grass glows where
a few small sprinklers still
bravely defy the crisping season of
heatwave and rainless smog.
Trees trimmed and cosseted still
joyfully offer shade, patiently
endure acid gingering at the
tip, and ache at the roots;
they'd had no choice between,
all winterlong, drinking or every toe
shrinking in slush and salt.

Brisk with his cane, a morning
walker sniffs – and slows.
Fresh loam! Aroma
out of the dawn of time.
The Parks truck is unpacking
this month's tenants for
the circular park-flower-bed,
northwest corner, just past
the traffic light.

Its youthful occupants were
iris, and tulips, once.
Today – marigolds?
Mid-season tenancy is claimed for the
begonias. But
oh, old age's final
occupancy, the
chrysanthemums!
(Never, at this
unquiet corner, the
delicate aster).

You who set out, not seed,
you yet make glad our hearts.

Nostrils, draw in deep!
Feast, dimmed but dreamy
eyes! Life digs its toes in
here too, and flourishes,

being cared for, and
about, by you
purposeful Parks employees.

Thanks

This book was kept in process by two friends, Stan Dragland and Joan Eichner, both sensitive editors. Their discernment, orderliness, patience, oh and e-mailing, saw it through to completion. I cannot thank them enough. Stan and Joan also did final editing for *Concrete and Wild Carrot.*

Here I remember Kathleen Coburn (the Coleridgean) whose intervention, in England, got my first book out, *Winter Sun,* put together thanks to an eight-month grant (1956) from the Guggenheim Foundation. The late Denise Levertov, at Norton's request for six manuscripts, sought out mine (*The Dumbfounding*). William Pope produced the next two volumes (*sunblue, No Time*) as his own venture, then *Not Yet But Still* with help from the Canada Council for the Arts and the Nova Scotia Department of Education. I am grateful to all.

Acknowledgements*

Magazines:

Acta Victoriana, Applegarth's Folly, Blew Ointment, Canadian Forum, Canadian Literature, Canadian Review, Canadian Woman Studies, The Catalyst, Chatelaine, Christianity Today, Combustion, Compass, Desert Review, Ganglia, Ellipse, Evidence, Exile, Hermes, His, The Human Voice, Image, IS, Island, Kenyon Review, The Literary Review, The Michigan Quarterly Review, The New Quarterly, The New Reasoner, Origin, Poetry Canada Review, Poetry (Chicago), *Presbyterian Record, Queen's Quarterly, Right On, The Second Mile, The* (Toronto) *Telegram.*

Anthologies (in chronological order):

A.J.M. Smith, ed. *The Book of Canadian Poetry: A Critical and Historical Anthology.* Chicago: University of Chicago Press; Toronto: Gage, 1943.
John Sutherland, ed. *Other Canadians: An Anthology of New Poetry in Canada 1940–1946.* Montreal: First Statement, 1947.
Louis Dudek and Irving Layton, eds. *Canadian Poems 1850–1952.* Toronto: Contact, 1952.
Earle Birney, ed. *Twentieth Century Canadian Poetry: An Anthology with Introduction and Notes.* Toronto: Ryerson, 1953.
Bliss Carman, Lorne Pierce, and V.B. Rhodenizer. *Canadian Poetry in English.* Foreword by Lorne Pierce. Toronto: Ryerson, 1954.
Ralph Gustafson, ed. *The Penguin Book of Canadian Verse.* Harmondsworth: Penguin, 1958.
A.J.M. Smith, ed. *The Oxford Book of Canadian Verse: In English and French.* Toronto: Oxford University Press, 1960.
Eli Mandel and Jean-Guy Pilon, eds. *Poetry 62.* Toronto: Ryerson, 1961.
Ilona Duczynska and Karl Polanyi, eds. *The Plough and the Pen: Writings from Hungary 1930–1956.* Foreword by W.H. Auden. Toronto: McClelland & Stewart, 1963.

---

* This list has been revised and expanded from that printed in Volumes One and Two.

Milton Wilson, ed. *The Poetry of Mid-Century 1940–1960*. Toronto: McClelland & Stewart, 1964.

Claude Bissell, ed. *Great Canadian Writing: A Century of Imagination*. Toronto: Canadian Centennial, 1966.

Gordon Green and Guy Sylvestre. *A Century of Canadian Literature/ Un Siècle de littérature canadienne*. Toronto: Ryerson, 1967.

Gary Geddes, ed. *20th Century Poetry & Poetics*. Toronto: Oxford University Press, 1969.

Gary Geddes and Phyllis Bruce, eds. *15 Canadian Poets*. Toronto: Oxford University Press, 1970.

Oscar Williams, ed. *A Little Treasury of Modern Poetry*. 3rd edn. New York: Scribners, 1970.

H. Houtman, ed. *Six Days: An Anthology of Canadian Christian Poetry*. Toronto: Wedge Publications, 1971.

Eli Mandel, ed. *Eight More Canadian Poets*. Toronto: Holt, Rinehart and Winston, 1972.

Homer Hogan, ed. *Listen! Songs and Poems of Canada*. Methuen Canadian Literature Series. Toronto: Methuen, 1972.

Richard Ellman and Robert O'Clair, eds. *The Norton Anthology of Modern Poetry*. New York: Norton, 1973.

Paul Denham, ed. Preface by Mary Jane Edwards. *The Evolution of Canadian Literature in English*. Toronto: Holt, Rinehart and Winston, 1973.

Robert Weaver, ed. *The Oxford Anthology of Canadian Literature*. Toronto: Oxford University Press, 1973.

Alvin Lee, Hope Arnott Lee, and W.T. Jewkes, eds. Supervising editor, Northrop Frye. *The Peaceable Kingdom*. Literature: Uses of the Imagination Series. New York: Harcourt, Brace, Jovanovich, 1974.

Carl F. Klinck and Reginald E. Watters, eds. *Canadian Anthology*. Toronto: Gage, 1974.

Herbert Barrows, Caesar R. Blake, Arthur J. Carr, Arthur M. Eastman, and Hubert M. English, eds. *The Norton Anthology of Poetry*. New York: Norton, 1975.

Cid Corman, ed. *The Gist of Origin*. New York: Grossman, 1975.

Gary Geddes and Phyllis Bruce, eds. *15 Canadian Poets Plus 5*. Toronto: Oxford University Press, 1978.

John Newlove, ed. *Canadian Poetry: The Modern Era*. Toronto: McClelland & Stewart, 1977.

Merle Meeter, ed. *The Country of the Risen King: An Anthology of*

Christian Poetry. Grand Rapids, Michigan: Baker Book House, 1978.
Douglas Daymond and Leslie Monkman, eds. *Literature in Canada*. Vol 11. Toronto: Gage, 1978.
John Frederic Nims, ed. *The Harper Anthology of Poetry*. New York: Harper, 1981.
August Kleinzahler, ed. *News and Weather: Seven Canadian Poets*. Ilderton, Ontario: Brick Books, 1982.
Jack David and Robert Lecker, eds. *Canadian Poetry*. Toronto/Downsview, Ontario: General/ECW, 1982.
Margaret Atwood, ed. *The New Oxford Book of Canadian Verse: In English*. Vol. 11. Toronto: Oxford University Press, 1983.
Donna Bennett and Russell Brown, eds. *An Anthology of Canadian Literature in English*. Vol. 11. Toronto: Oxford University Press, 1983.
In Celebration, Anemos. Poems for Denise Levertov on her sixtieth birthday. Palo Alto: Matrix Press, 1983.
Robert Lecker and Jack David, eds. *The New Canadian Anthology*. Toronto: Nelson, 1988.
Gary Geddes, ed. *15 Canadian Poets x 2*. Don Mills, Ontario: Oxford, 1988.
David A. Kent, ed. *Christian Poetry in Canada*. Toronto: ECW Press, 1989.
Gary Geddes, ed. *15 Canadian Poets x 3*. Don Mills, Ontario: Oxford, 2001.
Br. Quenon and John B. Lee, eds. *Smaller Than God*. Windsor, Ontario: Black Moss Press, 2001.
János Tarn and Katalin Thury, eds. *Kristálykert/Crystal Garden*. Budapest: Hungarian-Canadian Friendship Society, 2001.
Donna Bennett and Russell Brown, eds. *A New Anthology of Canadian Literature in English*. Don Mills, Ontario: Oxford University Press, 2002.
Sharon Thesen, ed. *The Griffin Poetry Prize Anthology: A Selection of the 2003 Shortlist*. Toronto: House of Anansi Press, 2003.
Robert Scholes, Nancy R. Comley, Carl H. Klaus, David Staines, eds. *Elements of Literature, Poetry/Fiction/Drama*. Don Mills, Ontario: Oxford University Press, 2004
Robert Stamp, ed. *Writing the Terrain: a poetry anthology*. Calgary: University of Calgary Press, 2004.
Kevin Prufer, ed. *Dark Horses: Poets on Overlooked Poems*. Champaign, Ill.: University of Illinois Press, 2005.
Herbert Rosengarten and Amanda Goldrick-Jones, eds. *The Broadview Anthology of Poetry*. 2nd ed. Calgary: Broadview Press, 2005.

Translations:

Branko Gorjup and Francesca Valente, eds. *Il cuore che vede/The Optic Eye*. Ravenna: Longo Editore, 2003.

Publishers:

Routledge & Kegan Paul, London, *Winter Sun*, 1960
W.W. Norton, New York, *The Dumbfounding*, 1966
McClelland & Stewart, Toronto, *Winter Sun and The Dumbfounding, Poems 1940–66*, 1982
Oxford University Press, Toronto, *Selected Poems*, 1991
Lancelot Press, Hantsport, Nova Scotia, *sunblue*, 1978; *No Time*, 1989; *Not Yet But Still*, 1997
Brick Books, London, Ontario, *Concrete and Wild Carrot*, 2002
The Porcupine's Quill, Erin, Ontario, *Always Now: Volume One*, 2003; *Always Now: Volume Two*, 2004.

Index of Titles

Aftermath of Rebellion   57
Air and Blood   32
Ajar   201
Alternative to Riots But All Citizens Must Play   179
Ambivalence   133
And If No Ram Appear   73
Artless Art   46
asap; etc.   30
Astonishing Reversal   68
Audrey: A Posthumous Portrait   138
Balancing Out   130
Basis, A   40
Because Your Hour Is Dark   199
Betrayed into Glory   205
Beyond Weather *or* From a Train Window   15
Breath Catching   78
But One Recoiled   198
Christmas Doubts Dissolved   81
Communication at Mortal Risk   44
Concert   65
Confrontation and Resolution, in *Job*   103
Contemplative Hour   18
Contextualizing, *or* Neither Here Nor There   177
Cosmosis   192
Cross-Cultural *or* Towards Burnout   48
Crux, The   131
Cultures Far and Here   50
Cycle of Community   156
Dead Ends   159
Dividing Goods   127
Early Easter Sunday Morning Radio   195
Embrace Change?   77
End Not Yet, The   204
Endangerer, The   170
Ex-Communicants   198

Familiar Friend, But by the Ottawa River, The   66
Family Members   54
Fixed in a Flux, The   185
For a Salty and Sainted Friend in Her Nineties   59
Four Words: A Gloss on I Cor. 14: 6   173
From Now – On?   16
He Was There/He Was Here   143
How Open, Who Are Compassed Here?   63
'I Wondered As I Wandered'   206
In Our 'Little Nests'   176
In Season and out of Season   69
Instrumentalists Rehearse   100
Interim   85
It Isn't Really True? (in Four Voices)   90
Kept Secret, A   96
Knowing the New   28
Lament for Byways   161
Late Perspective   34
Leading Questions   166
Lit Sky and Foundered Earth   19
Loam   208
Making a Living   31
Music Was in the Wind   42
Nahuatl/ *Tomana* (to Swell)   191
Ne Cedere: 'Won't Go Away'   187
News Item   99
Not Quite Silently   21
Notes from Dr Carson's Exposition of I John 5   142
Old Woman at a Winter Window   15
On a Maundy Thursday Walk   174
'One Rule of Modesty and Soberness'   86
Open   197
Other Oceans   146
Pacing the Turn of the Year   119
Peculiarity: Local Loyalties, A   39
Poring   45
Potentiality   37
Prairie Poem   125

Present from Ted   122
Prodded out of Prayer   76
Prospecting   160
Proving   79
Ramsden   129
Relating   135
Remembering Gordon G. Nanos   144
Resolute Lament   190
Responses   137
Resting on a Dry Log, Park Bench, Boulder   97
Reversing a Crater   139
Rising Dust   163
Risk of No Communication, The   52
Sad Song   203
Seed of History, A   93
Seer, Seeing   60
Seriously?   158
Shelter?   95
Slow Advance   23
Strolling   202
Sultry Day   29
'Tell them everything that I command …'   35
That Friday – Good?   84
There Are No Words For   25
Third Hand, First Hand   141
Thought in a Sick-Room   20
Three Bears   101
Three Shore Breakfasts   196
To Counter Malthus   72
To Wilfred Cantwell Smith   171
Too Towards Tomorrow   189
Towards the Next Change   124
Transition   47
Two   165
Two Perilous Possibilities   82
Uncircular   167
We Are Not Desecrators   36
What John Saw   74

When Their Little Girl Had Just Died   26
When the Bough Breaks   27
Whole Story, The   155
Women's Poem: Now, A   55
Women's Poem: Then and Now, A   56
Word: Russets   94

JOAN EICHNER

Margaret Avison was born in Galt, Ontario, in 1918. She studied at the University of Toronto, and subsequently worked as a librarian, editor, lecturer, and social worker. She has twice been awarded the Governor General's Award (for *Winter Sun*, 1960, and *No Time*, 1989). She holds three honorary doctorates, and has been named an Officer of the Order of Canada. Her most recent collection of poems, *Concrete and Wild Carrot* (Brick Books, 2002), was awarded the Griffin Prize for Poetry. It also received the Jack Chalmers Poetry Award from the Canadian Authors Association.